"Over dinner in their home, Margaret and Dwight Peterson regaled me with stories from their class at Eastern. As I sat there, knowing that a class I teach touches on the themes they spoke of, I kept thinking, 'This needs to be put into a book.' That hope is now realized in this book. Christians have so many confusing ideas about marriage. This is the place to begin for a no-nonsense approach, biblical thinking and theological explanation. Give this book to everyone thinking about marriage and to every young couple (and to confused veterans of marriage)."

SCOT MCKNIGHT, Karl A. Olsson Professor in Religious Studies, North Park University

"Eureka—I have found it! Amid all the crass, consumerist Christian books on sex, romance and married life, finally we're treated to a realistic portrait of life and love in all its beauty and frustration. With a refreshing penchant for acknowledging the dilemmas that real people confront as they hope for marriage, marry and grow old together—or not—the Petersons gently name and confront what young and old face today. This book is honest, unflinching, faithful and worth reading every page. I would be a wiser man, husband and father today if I could've read it twenty years ago."

MARK REGNERUS, associate professor of sociology, University of Texas at Austin, and author of *Premarital Sex in America*

"For years I've been looking for a book I could give friends who are getting married—something that sums up the complex gift and challenge that Christian marriage is. Finally, I've found it. The Petersons combine the skills of a theologian and a Bible scholar with the experience of both being married and helping students prepare for marriage. Here is a book full of good sense and good news. I'm sending it to two friends n

JONATHAN WILSON

(www.jonathanwi

v monastic

Margaret Kim Peterson
& Dwight N. Peterson

Are You Waiting for "The One"?

Cultivating Realistic, Positive

Expectations for Christian Marriage

IVP Books

An imprint of InterVarsity Press
Downers Grove, Illinois

InterVarsity Press
P.O. Box 1400, Downers Grove, IL 60515-1426
World Wide Web: www.ivpress.com
E-mail: email@ivpress.com

InterVarsity Press® is the book-publishing division of InterVarsity Christian Fellowship/USA®, a movement of students and faculty active on campus at hundreds of universities, colleges and schools of nursing in the United States of America, and a member movement of the International Fellowship of Evangelical Students. For information about local and regional activities, write Public Relations Dept., InterVarsity Christian Fellowship/USA, 6400 Schroeder Rd., P.O. Box 7895, Madison, WI 53707-7895, or visit the IVCF website at <www.intervarsity.org>.

The Scripture quotations quoted herein are from the Revised Standard Version of the Bible, copyright 1946, 1952, 1971 by the Division of Christian Education of the National Council of the Churches of Christ in the U.S.A. Used by permission. All rights reserved.

While all stories in this book are true, some names and identifying information in this book have been changed to protect the privacy of the individuals involved.

Design: Cindy Kiple
Images: scroll design: © GARY GODBY/iStockphoto
        illustration of a couple walking: Bull's Eye/Getty Images

ISBN 978-0-8308-3310-8

Printed in the United States of America ∞

 InterVarsity Press is committed to protecting the environment and to the responsible use of natural resources. As a member of Green Press Initiative we use recycled paper whenever possible. To learn more about the Green Press Initiative, visit <www.greenpressinitiative.org>.

Library of Congress Cataloging-in-Publication Data

Peterson, Margaret Kim, 1961-
  Are you waiting for "the one"?: cultivating realistic, positive
expectations for Christian marriage / Margaret Kim Peterson and Dwight
N. Peterson.
     p. cm.
  Includes bibliographical references.
  ISBN 978-0-8308-3310-8 (pbk.: alk. paper)
  1. Marriage—Religious aspects—Christianity. 2. Spouses—Religious
life. I. Peterson, Dwight N. II. Title.
  BV4596.M3P48 2011
  248.8'44—dc22
                                                            2011006804

P   18   17   16   15   14   13   12   11   10   9   8   7   6   5   4   3   2   1
Y   26   25   24   23   22   21   20   19   18   17   16   15   14   13   12   11

Contents

Preface

THIS BOOK HAD ITS BEGINNINGS in a college course that we began teaching more than a decade ago. Marriage was a topic of interest to us—as teachers of Christian Scripture and theology, as members of a local church and of other social and familial communities, and simply as human beings—and we hoped that there might be students at our institution who would be interested in reflecting with us on that subject.

By its second offering the course had grown in popularity to the point that we had to limit it to seniors only. That limitation has itself shaped the class in fundamental ways. Graduation from college is in modern American society a primary marker of the transition to adulthood, and marriage has at least in the past functioned as another such marker. College seniors are thus poised to think about marriage in newly adult ways, to consider how their lives to that point have been shaped by their familial and other relationships, and to consider whether and with whom they might wish to embark upon the married life themselves.

From the inception of the course, we have tried very hard to listen at least as much as we talk. To ensure that there is something for us to listen to, we ask our students to write short essays for us most weeks. The requirement is only that class members reflect in writing on the subject matter of the course. They do not have to talk about themselves, but they are welcome to do so if they like. We want to know what they are thinking, so that the course can be a conversation about matters of mutual concern rather than being shaped only by our own ideas or experiences.

We were both honored and taken aback, the first time we taught this course, by the torrent of very personal storytelling that this essay requirement unleashed. We are used to it now, but we are no less honored every year to make the acquaintance of a new group of students and to be offered glimpses into their personal lives and the questions and challenges confronting them as Christian young people just entering adulthood.

Those essays and their stories have become an integral element of the class. As we read each weekly batch of essays, we take notes, and we begin the next week's class by talking about the previous week's essays—noting common themes, retelling particularly striking stories, quoting particularly memorable passages, and in all of this, allowing the members of the class to collaborate with us and with each other in creating a conversation about marriage and Christian faith and the Christian life in general.

We have done the same thing in this book, which includes some of those striking stories and memorable passages and draws upon countless other comments made by class members either in writing or in class discussion. As is our practice in class, when we retell a story, we always omit or alter any identifying details. We also sometimes edit a person's remarks for grammar or style rather than quoting him or her precisely. But none of the stories and words that we repeat in this book are our own invention. Real people really did say these things, and this book represents an effort to continue the conversation by putting those remarks and the experiences from which they arise in a theological and cultural-critical context that is helpfully illuminating.

When we teach our course, we talk about our own stories as

well. Our marriage is a second marriage for both of us. Dwight was divorced from his first wife, and the fact of his divorce has helped us and our students to avoid the facile moralism that too often characterizes Christian conversation about divorce, and instead to explore honestly and openly what it means to fail, to need grace, and to receive it in the context of the church and of one's own life.

Margaret was a widow when she married Dwight; she was happily married the first time around, and is now happily married a second time. This aspect of her experience runs counter to a cultural assumption that we have come to call the "myth of the one true love": the notion that there is exactly one right person out there for everyone, and that the task of the person who wishes to marry is to identify, woo and win (or be wooed and won by) the one true love.

Many, if not most, of our students have been influenced by the myth of the one true love to the point that they are mystified by Margaret's two marriages. They wonder which of her husbands was the one true love, and how Dwight can stand to be married to someone who might ever have truly loved someone else. These questions have helped us and our students think through what it means both to love and to grieve, experiences that are central in the lives of most people, whether married or not.

Of course there is more to our stories than our marital histories. In the course of any given semester, we explore those stories in some detail with our students, as we do our best to model what it might look like to reflect honestly and thoughtfully and with good humor upon our small stories in the light of that great story that is the gospel of Christ crucified and risen.

In this book, however, it is our students and their stories who take center stage, as they and we reflect together on their experiences of life and relationship in that same light. We are enormously grateful to all the men and women who have been our conversation partners. We hope that both their and our contributions to that conversation will come together to make a book that will be thought provoking and helpful to many others.

1

Young Love

Beyond the Fantasy of Romance

THERE WAS A TIME, not so very long ago, when a great many Americans who got married did so at the very beginning of their adult lives. In the 1960s, the median age at first marriage was 22.8 for men and 20.3 for women. Fifty years later, it is hard to imagine a world in which nearly half of all first-time brides are teenagers. By 2010 the median age at first marriage had risen to 28.2 for men and 26.1 for women, the highest it had ever been since the U.S. Census Bureau started keeping records in 1890.[1]

This move toward later marriage is part of a larger trend toward later adulthood in general. Changes in the global economy and in the American educational and employment sectors have made establishing an independent household and settling into a career a much longer process than it was just a generation or two ago. Jobs requiring only a high school education do not yield paychecks that can support a family. Going to college can easily involve more than four years and more than one institution. Graduation from college is often followed by a decade or more of student loan repayment, and many desirable career paths require yet more school-

---

[1] www.census.gov/population/socdemo/hh-fam/ms2.csv.

ing and yet more loans, leaving no time and no money for things like marriage and child rearing.

The result in the culture at large is a sense that marriage, which often used to be a first step into adulthood, is now properly the last. The right time to marry, so the thought goes, is after you have had every other desirable adult experience: education, travel, work and lots of relationships with lots of different people. You should certainly be no younger than twenty-five, and even then it might be well to wait. It is fine to be "in a relationship" as a young person, but marriage is something best saved for a later stage in one's life.

A different ideal holds sway among at least some Christians. "The expected schedule of events is this," writes one woman. "Graduate from high school, go to college, meet the love of your life, get engaged, graduate in May and get married in June." Why the rush? A young man explains: "I think most Christians believe that singleness is not an option for Christians, either as a way to serve God or as a way to be happy." The implication is obvious: if singleness is not an option, then marriage is a duty, and you had best get on with it as soon as possible.

It's not as easy as it sounds. In fact, it is not easy at all. It is challenging to make sense of these conflicting cultural and ideological pressures. Is it really true that young people have no business getting married? Is it really true that Christians are supposed to get married? And it is not easy to value and pursue genuinely Christian relationships of any sort in a social context that increasingly values technology and change over human connection and faithfulness. So what do you do? Where do you turn for assistance and advice?

A possible resource might be Christian romantic advice literature.[2] Unfortunately, a lot of this really isn't very helpful. Many of

---

[2]See, for example, John Eldredge, *Wild at Heart: Discovering the Secret of a Man's Soul* (Nashville: Thomas Nelson, 2006); John Eldredge and Staci Eldredge, *Captivating: Unveiling the Mystery of a Woman's Soul* (Nashville: Thomas Nelson, 2005); Joshua

these books are written by very young people whose strength is that they have experienced firsthand the challenging cultural realities facing Christian young people today. Their weakness is that the alternative they propose is an utterly unrealistic romantic fantasy that owes nothing to the gospel and everything to Disneyland and Madison Avenue. Are there better options? Are there ways to be honest about the challenges of the Christian life and of Christian relationships, and to open doors to the kind of real love that can stand the test of time?

Yes, there are. In this chapter we will look first at contemporary cultural patterns of relationship and then at the supposedly Christian ideal of relationship presented in many romantic advice books as an alternative to this. And then we will consider another way—what it might mean to look not for perfect love but for real love.

The Bad News

The authors of Christian romantic advice books are right about one thing: this is a hard world in which to form authentic and meaningful relationships. Ten years ago, a term current among our students was "friends with benefits." As semiclueless members of an older generation, we had to ask for an explanation: it meant, our students told us, the practice of having sexual relations, or the next thing to them, with people with whom one was otherwise "just friends."

Ripples of embarrassed giggles spread over the lecture hall as our students educated us on this topic, which was, it ap-

Harris, *I Kissed Dating Goodbye: A New Attitude Toward Romance and Relationships* (Sisters, Ore.: Multnomah, 1997); Harris, *Boy Meets Girl: Say Hello to Courtship* (Sisters, Ore.: Multnomah, 2000); Eric Ludy and Leslie Ludy, *When God Writes Your Love Story: The Ultimate Approach to Guy/Girl Relationships* (Sisters, Ore.: Loyal, 1999); Leslie Ludy, *Authentic Beauty: The Shaping of a Set-Apart Young Woman* (Sisters, Ore.: Multnomah, 2003); Heather Arnel Paulsen, *Emotional Purity: An Affair of the Heart* (Wheaton, Ill.: Crossway, 2007).

peared, foreign to no one, although the degree of students' personal involvement in such activities varied considerably. It didn't seem so funny the next week, however, when one woman showed up in class with eyes swollen from weeping, on the verge of yet more tears. Her younger brother, who was still in high school, had disclosed to her and their parents the night before that not only had he gotten a girl pregnant but also that the relationship in the context of which this pregnancy had occurred was not even one of particular intimacy. They were just "friends with benefits."

The notion of "friends with benefits" now seems positively quaint. It has been replaced by the hookup culture, in which one has sexual relations, or the next thing to them, with perfect strangers. This phenomenon is described in books like *Unhooked*, which focuses on how sexual activity among high school and college-age young women is increasingly decoupled from anything resembling intimate relationship.[3] It should perhaps go without saying that, among heterosexuals at least, the involvement of men in the hookup culture is just as great as that of women, although it is possible that the effects of that culture on men may be different in detail from its effects on women.

It is difficult to believe, however, that the hookup culture is anything but bad for anyone, male or female. The more casual sexual behavior becomes, the less it serves to deepen existing intimacy and the more it becomes a substitute for and even an impediment to intimacy. After all, if you begin by falling into bed with someone, what could you possibly gain by getting to know him or her afterward? And the pleasures and costs of hooking up turn out to be rather like those of pornography: the pleasure is increasingly fleeting and shallow, and the costs come due eventu-

---

[3]Laura Sessions Stepp, *Unhooked: How Young Women Pursue Sex, Delay Love and Lose at Both* (New York: Riverhead, 2007).

ally in the guise of a corroded and misshapen capacity for genuine relationship with anyone.

It is no wonder, then, that the authors of Christian romantic advice books take so dim a view of the contemporary social scene, and that their books find a ready audience among Christian young people, who see in themselves and in others the damage wrought by unwise sexual involvement and who long for something better. What is not always so evident, either to these authors or to their readers, are the ways in which contemporary Christian culture inadvertently contributes to and participates in the world of the hookup.

Make no mistake about it: Christians are part of this phenomenon. A good many Christian young people are not simply scandalized observers of the hookup culture, but are themselves participants in it. Again the analogy with pornography is pertinent. Business analysts have shown that in hotel rooms in which pay-per-view porn is available (and that is now the case in the majority of mid-level to high-end hotels), more than half of all guests pay to view the porn.[4] The use of pornography, in other words, has become more common than not.

And so it is with casual sexual behavior among Christian young people. There are of course some young men and women who live very chastely. But there are others at the opposite end of the spectrum, and the majority are somewhere in the middle, behaving in ways that to their elders would undoubtedly seem shockingly loose but that in the social milieu inhabited by these young people are so common as to seem almost inevitable.

This seeming inevitability of casual and otherwise nonmarital sexual behavior is a sad indictment of the Christian formation that contemporary Christian young people are receiving—or not

---

[4]Timothy Egan, "Erotica Inc.," *New York Times*, October 23, 2000.

receiving—in their churches and homes. What is typically absent from that formation is any attempt to grapple in truthful and theologically substantive ways with contemporary social realities. The result is young people who may know what is expected of them, but who are unable to think of any persuasive reason to meet those expectations.

This phenomenon was illustrated for us vividly by a woman who asked—half sheepishly, half defiantly—if we could explain to her precisely why she should not move in with her boyfriend upon graduation. "I know it's wrong," she said, "but everybody does it, and it would be so much more convenient. And if we don't live together officially, he'll end up spending the night anyway. Why should we go to the trouble and expense of setting up two separate apartments? Who would we think we were kidding?"

Along with the absence of creative theological engagement with contemporary realities, there is typically present in much Christian rhetoric about sex a great deal of emphasis on virginity and "waiting." But here again the result too often is not to *counter* cultural mores regarding sexual behavior but rather to inadvertently *reinforce* them. Talking about sex primarily as something to be waited for encourages a passivity in young people that tends not to be able to withstand the tug of broader cultural forces.

It also encourages the equation of sexual maturity with sexual activity. Mature manhood and womanhood are not presented as states people have the opportunity to grow into gradually, whether or not they ever marry or engage in sexual relations. The assumption appears rather to be that one will remain a child until he or she begins having sex, and that Christians ought to wait until they are married both for sex and for adult status.

It is unsurprising, therefore, that many Christian young people resent being shunted into singles' groups that seem to function as holding pens for those who are not yet allowed to join the grown-ups, and equally unsurprising that most of them do not, in fact, "wait for marriage." In a society fraught with divorce and in which the securing of a marriage partner is exclusively the responsibility of the individual, marriage can seem impossibly distant and risky. Sex, on the other hand, is readily available, whether with someone you know or with someone you don't. So why wait for marriage, when you can have the benefits of sex right now?

There is another more subtle way in which contemporary Christian attitudes toward sex and commitment mirror rather than contrast those of society at large. Part of the appeal of the hookup culture is that it offers the pleasure of sex without the danger of commitment. Commitment is dangerous, so the thought goes, partly because of the possibility of a breakup, but also because commitment limits one's options. A person who is sincerely attached to a boyfriend or girlfriend might allow that relationship to influence decisions about education or career, and might as a result not succeed or achieve as much as he or she might have otherwise. It is permissible, therefore, to pursue sex, but love must at all costs be delayed, lest some premature commitment derail one's life or career.

Counterintuitive though it may seem, there are many contemporary Christians who share this sense that young people should avoid getting too tied down, too soon. The difference is only in what is seen as "too tied down." The hookup culture sees any relationship at all as too tied down. What is left of the dating culture sees early marriage as too tied down. The Christian culture sees parenthood as too tied down. If young people want to have sex, they can get married, but they mustn't have babies until they are "ready." What counts as "ready" varies: done with college, done with graduate school, established in a career, financially secure, perhaps just simply older than they are now. Most fundamentally, they need to be in a place in which having a child will not unduly restrict their options.

Most of our students are not married, but in the lives of nearly everyone who is, we see evidence of this deep cultural bias against young parenthood. There are the young husbands and wives who long for a baby but say they feel they must wait because their parents, while delighted with their marriage, would be horrified if they got pregnant. There are the married women who are terrified that they might become pregnant, because, they say, it would be disastrous if they did. The women who do conceive, or the men whose wives become pregnant, typically view the event with dismay: there were so many things they wanted to do before they had children, and now they won't be able to do them.

And then there is the story told by a woman whose close friend, still in her early twenties, had had a baby at some respectable interval after being married. The friend had described, with some bitterness, her sense that her fellow church members disapproved of her young married motherhood more than they disapproved even of unwed motherhood. After all, an unwed mother could be patronizingly dismissed as having made a mistake, whereas she, a married woman, had evidently done this on purpose.

What a good many contemporary Christians seem to have lost sight of is that Christians have traditionally understood marriage, sex and children as things that properly go together. Marriages are meant to be fruitful, and in the absence of modern contraceptive methods, most marriages are, and in fairly short order. But we live in a contraceptive culture, one in which the good baby is a responsibly planned baby, and whose appearance on the scene is the result of a completely different set of decisions from the decision to get married.

The result too often is Christians who see marriage as a church-sanctioned form of fairy-tale romance. Marriage, in this view, makes sex respectable. But married sex is not supposed to result in babies any more than unmarried sex is, at least not until the young couple is not so young anymore. Why not? Well, because young love is supposed to be unfettered and carefree; it is supposed to be characterized by romantic getaways and lacy lingerie, not by night feedings and decisions whether to use cloth or disposable diapers.

And in this exaltation of romance, understood as something quite separate from—and indeed likely to be impaired by—parenthood, too many Christians come perilously close to endorsing an ideal of relationship that differs only in the presence of a wedding ring from the ideal of relationship found in the broader culture. Get married, Christian parents and relationship advisors urge Christian young people, but when you get married, be sure that what you are getting is a fairy tale, a romance that fulfills your desires for intimacy while leaving you free to pursue whatever other goals you may have. And whatever you do, don't get pregnant on your honeymoon!

Perfect Love

Christian romantic advice givers tend not to notice these correlations between secular patterns of relationship and what Christians think and do. They see the undeniable damage that results when sexual behavior is separated from relational intimacy, and when relationships of whatever degree of intimacy follow one another in rapid succession rather than enduring faithfully over time, and they prescribe an alternate Christian ideal: a romantic fantasy whose focus is a phenomenon we might call perfect love.

Perfect love has exactly one object: the mate whom God has chosen for you, otherwise known as the one true love, or just "the one." You don't have to wonder whether this person is right for you, because this person is God's choice, not yours. You don't have to risk a possible breakup, or suffer through an actual breakup, because God guarantees the success of the relationship. Perfect love comes with all the benefits of romance and none of the drawbacks.

Perfect love is, well, perfect. There is never a hint of compromise. No one need settle for less than he or she deserves, and everyone deserves only the best. She is beautiful; he is handsome. She is thin; he is muscular. She plays the piano; he plays the guitar. Both parties embody every item on the other's list of desirable qualities in a spouse, a list that each of them has been keeping since he or she was twelve.

Perfect love is dramatic. When she first catches sight of him, she thinks, *Wow!* When his eyes first meet hers, sparks fly. Their developing relationship is filled with romantic dinners for two, exchanges of thoughtful little gifts, maybe a short-term mission trip to an exotic locale. He and she are at center stage all of the time since, after all, they are the stars. His proposal is creative and personal and romantic; everybody who hears about it is impressed and envious.

Perfect love is smooth sailing. Everyone is healthy; everyone's family is pious and untroubled and supportive. The couple themselves are unambiguously happy all of the time. If conflicts or hurt feelings related to past romantic or sexual entanglements arise, these are dealt with in the space of ten or fifteen minutes at most. Otherwise the couple never fight, because they have God at the center of their relationship, they are clear about their biblical roles as a man and woman, and, after all, they love each other.

Perfect love always comes with plenty of money. Flowers, candlelit dinners and extravagant gestures abound, showing the world that he loves her. On Valentine's Day in particular, all these things, plus chocolate, are an absolute necessity. Any woman who is offered less is justified in feeling herself severely wronged, and any woman who would settle for less is likely to be chastised by her friends for not holding out for more.

Perfect love finds its climax in a perfect wedding, which is necessarily an elaborate affair. The complexity of planning such a wedding is offset somewhat by the fact that the bride has been planning it since before she met the groom; in fact, planning her wedding was a required senior project at the private Christian high school she attended. Of course the wedding is expensive; the bride's friends must spend a small fortune for the privilege of being bridesmaids, but they are presumed willing to do this because, after all, perfect love deserves a perfect wedding.

In the wedding ceremony, the friends of the bride and groom testify to the fairy-tale nature of the bridal couple's romance. In his sermon the minister does the same. At the reception the bride and groom are introduced as the prince and princess of the day, and at the close of the festivities they are borne off to the airport for the start of a honeymoon in a remote and sunny location, ready to embrace the blissful and cloudless future that God prepares for those who wait on him.

We are not making any of this up. Over and over again our students tell us that this is what they have been taught by their elders and their peers to want and expect in a relationship. A good many of these things we have found explicitly stated in one Christian romantic advice book or another. And these books are very clear: this is all of God. God is the author of romance, and if you allow God to shape your destiny, perfect love will be your reward.

How do you get this to happen for you? The books tell us that too. What is needed, they say, is a Christian alternative to "dating." Particularly in more conservative social and religious settings where the utter anomie of the hookup culture has not yet taken hold, dating is the defining emotional experience in the lives of many young people. Adolescence has become a time of constant cycling in and out of temporarily exclusive intimate relationships, each of which is characterized by intense emotional—and sometimes physical—attachment and followed, when it ends, by intense disappointment, disillusionment and despair.

Dating, in other words, is all about falling in love and then falling out of love. The falling-in-love part is fun; the falling-out-of-love part is not. Isn't there a way, ask our romantic advice givers, to have the falling-in-love part without the falling-out-of-love part? Indeed there is. What you need to do is to stop dating all the wrong people. You need to stop trusting your own judgment where your love life is concerned, and start trusting God.

Trusting God with your love life means that you refrain from pursuing a romantic relationship with anyone unless and until God reveals to you that a particular person is "the one," the perfect partner whom God has been preparing for you from before the foundation of the world. God wants romance for you, and in God's own time he will provide the perfect partner. Until then, the pious Christian will watch and wait and hope and not date.

So what exactly do you do? The plan seems to be as follows. First, you isolate yourself from any deeply intimate emotional attachment to anyone but God. Second, you imagine in detail what your future partner is like and what your relationship with him or her will be. And third, when God does bring that special someone into your life, you recognize this person as your future mate through a kind of spiritual intuition that can be summed up in three words: "You just know."

The appeal of the first piece of this advice, the isolation of the self from emotional attachment to others, is that it holds out the promise that one will not suffer the disappointment and pain that comes with broken relationships. If you don't get close, you can't get hurt. This is not uncommon advice in Christian circles, even apart from discussions of love and marriage: people are fallible, and they will let you down, but God will never let you down. So don't trust in people; trust only in God.

To a generation of young people growing up ever more isolated from substantive relationships with their family members due to the combined effects of factors like ever-longer working hours, ever-fewer family meals, and the proliferation of computers and televisions to the point that there is at least one in every room of the house, this sounds like simple realism. If you are going to have emotional intimacy, it is going to have to be with God alone.

And yet people do long for emotional intimacy with other human beings. In the world of Christian romantic advice, this longing is precisely the same as the longing for marriage. Intimacy is by definition romantic, and people are allowed exactly two intimate relationships in their lives: the first with God, the second with the (future) spouse. In fact, emotional intimacy with anyone other than one's spouse constitutes unfaithfulness to the spouse. Just as Christians should save themselves physically for marriage by remaining sexually pure, so they should save themselves emotionally for marriage by not giving away pieces of their hearts to casual boyfriends or girlfriends.

The second recommendation offered to seekers of Christian romance—that they form a detailed imaginary portrait of what they are looking for in a spouse and in a marriage—is often accompanied by a very concrete suggestion: write it all down, in lists of desiderata and in letters to the future object of your affections. The point of doing so is itself threefold. First, it will help keep your romantic standards as high as God's are, and thus prevent you from settling for less than you want and deserve in a mate. Second, it will give you something to do on romantic occasions like Valentine's Day (instead of being depressed because you have not yet met "the one," you can instead write love letters to him or her). And, third, the accumulated cache of lists and letters can be presented to your future spouse on your wedding night as evidence of your premarital faithfulness: you did not spend your single years loving other people, but instead were busy looking forward to a life of bliss with your as-yet-unknown future mate.

The third step in letting God take charge of your love life involves the intuitive recognition of someone you do not yet know very well as "the one." Somewhere deep inside yourself, in a place to which only you have access, and in a way that makes it impossible to describe or explain to anyone else the grounds of your confidence, you just know that this is the future spouse whom God has chosen for you, and are thus liberated and empowered to pursue a romantic relationship with him or her.

The insistence of romantic advice authors on the ineffability of this certainty mirrors the tendency in broad swaths of Christian culture to believe that the less able one is to put things into words, the more deeply one must feel those things. This is true of prayer, with traditional set forms ("Almighty God, unto whom all hearts are open, all desires known, and from whom no secrets are hid, cleanse the thoughts of our hearts by the inspiration of thy Holy Spirit, that we may perfectly love thee and worthily magnify thy holy name, through Christ our Lord, Amen") suspected of shallowness and insincerity and rejected in favor of contemporary praise-service-style prayer ("Father God, we just want to praise you, um, Father God . . ."), which by reason of its very vacuity is seen as profound and heartfelt.

And so it also is where romance is concerned. If one could give cogent reasons for believing that a certain person is "the one," this would itself constitute evidence to the contrary. It would suggest that one is thinking rather than feeling, and that one is expressing one's own will and desires rather than trusting in God to provide and to direct one's steps. Only by refusing to make your own decisions can you make room for God to act in your life and lead you to perfect love with the perfect partner.

It should be obvious by now how problematic this all is. There is no such thing as perfect love. People are not perfect, and their love stories are not perfect. And God is not in the business of handing people romantic fantasies fit for the Hollywood screen, on the condition that they resign all responsibility for their own lives. Christian faithfulness involves thinking and doing, and the fruit of faithfulness is much more interesting than any stock screenplay.

Most fundamentally, the fantasy of romance is rooted in a story different from the Christian story. The fantasy of romance assumes that the basic human problem is loneliness, and it prescribes romantic love as the remedy. Once you meet and marry "the one," your problems are solved. You are perfect, your partner is perfect, your relationship is perfect—all the two of you need from one another is "intimacy," and the two of you together stand in no need of anything from anyone else. Romance has saved you both out of your single loneliness and launched you into a future in which you have no needs that are not already fulfilled by one another.

The Christian story starts from what seems a similar place: the alienation of people from one another and from God. But in a Christian understanding, the human predicament goes far deeper than the longing felt by a person who might like to be married but isn't, and the remedy goes much further than the provision of matchmaking services to the pious. Charles Wesley, in his hymn "Jesus, Lover of My Soul," suggests a few aspects of human neediness and the remedies with which God in Christ meets those needs: sin is met with forgiveness, death with life, sickness with healing, weakness with strength, faint-heartedness with encouragement, defenselessness with protection, despair with hope.[5]

What he does not mention in this hymn is either singleness or marriage (one or both of which would undoubtedly be the subject of a hymn of this title, were it to be written today). The Christian tradition simply has never seen singleness as among the fundamental problems of humanity, nor marriage as among the primary benefits of redemption. Indeed, there have been seasons in the church's life in which it has been difficult for Christians to see the positive value that marriage does have in the economy of God. In certain sectors of the contemporary church, however, it seems that the pendulum has swung to the other extreme, with marriage viewed as the central means by which people are saved out of what would otherwise be a life of unbearable alienation.

It is thus profoundly ironic that the lens through which many modern Christians have come to interpret marriage—namely, the fantasy of romance—turns out to be so splintering and isolating a

---

[5]Jesus, lover of my soul, let me to Thy bosom fly,
While the nearer waters roll, while the tempest still is high.
Hide me, O my Savior, hide, till the storm of life is past;
Safe into the haven guide; O receive my soul at last.

Other refuge have I none, hangs my helpless soul on Thee;
Leave, ah! leave me not alone, still support and comfort me.
All my trust on Thee is stayed, all my help from Thee I bring;
Cover my defenseless head with the shadow of Thy wing.

Wilt Thou not regard my call? Wilt Thou not accept my prayer?
Lo! I sink, I faint, I fall—Lo! on Thee I cast my care;
Reach me out Thy gracious hand! While I of Thy strength receive,
Hoping against hope I stand, dying, and behold, I live.

Thou, O Christ, art all I want, more than all in Thee I find;
Raise the fallen, cheer the faint, heal the sick, and lead the blind.
Just and holy is Thy Name, I am all unrighteousness;
False and full of sin I am; Thou art full of truth and grace.

Plenteous grace with Thee is found, grace to cover all my sin;
Let the healing streams abound; make and keep me pure within.
Thou of life the fountain art, freely let me take of Thee;
Spring Thou up within my heart; rise to all eternity.

phenomenon. Romance, through its exclusive focus on the one true love, ends up separating people two by two from any other substantive human relationship. And as the sociologists tell us, it is in part that very separation from supportive networks of friends and family that makes many modern marriages as brittle and prone to collapse as they are.

Real Love

Perhaps what contemporary Christians need is less romance and more love—and we mean real love, not "perfect love." Real love is unitive and community forming; it weaves people together into familial and churchly networks of mutual care and dependence on one another and on God. Husbands and wives, neighbors and friends, children and grandchildren, widows and orphans, all are adopted by God into the household of the church and invited to love and care for one another in ways that certainly include the bond of marriage, but include as well a range of other human relationships—all of which involve real connection, real intimacy, real enjoyment of other people and a real participation in the redemptive work of God in the world.

Real love has more than one possible object, which means that you do not have to wait for love until you meet your future marriage partner. Intimacy is bigger than romance, and marital love has enough in common with other human loves that you can practice on people like your parents, your siblings, your neighbors and your friends. And the more you practice, the better off you will be. People learn to love precisely by loving and by being loved. You will be much better equipped to learn to love a spouse if you have had practice ahead of time in knowing and being deeply known by others.

Real love grows through use. You do not have to worry that if you spread it around, you will run out. Nor do you have to worry that if you enter into an intimate friendship with someone whom you do not end up marrying, that person will abscond with part of your heart and there will be less of you than there was before. If you hope to marry someone and do not, of course you will be disappointed. But a great deal of the pain of heartbreak comes not from disappointment in love, but because partners have not, in fact, treated one another lovingly. If you and your friend really do love each other, and really do treat each other well, you will grow in and through the relationship, whether or not it moves toward marriage.

Real love develops into deep, meaningful intensity. It does not start with it. The time to look for sparks to fly is after you know one another well enough actually to mean something to one another. When real love is dramatic, it is less like the overproduced, spotlit drama of the Broadway musical, and more like the drama of a neighborhood theater production—homemade, improvisational, full of laughter and the pleasure that comes of making something for one another.

Real love assumes that you are not perfect, and neither are any of the people you know. In a culture that encourages us to demand perfection in everything and everyone, this can seem very counter-intuitive. We live in a consumer society in which, we are told, we can have exactly what we want if only we are willing to shop long enough. But even where consumer goods are concerned this is seldom true, and where relationships are concerned it is never true. The fantasy of perfect love, with its insistence that we settle for nothing less than perfection, thus requires that we believe a lie.

Real love, by contrast, allows us to tell the truth. Giving up the quest for the perfect mate is not equivalent to "settling," if by settling we mean settling for second best. Giving up the quest for the perfect mate can mean an embrace of the truly best: the truth that while you are not perfect, you might be the right person for someone else, and that someone else, while not perfect, might be the right person for you. Real love invites us to look at the woman or man who bears no resemblance to the photoshopped models on magazine covers and see the real beauty of the real woman, the real strength of the real man, the real qualities of character and personality that could make this person a wonderful match for you.

Real love has room for the fact that life is not perfect, either. Perhaps your family is seriously troubled. Perhaps you have an illness or a disability. Perhaps you are strapped for cash or burdened with debt. Perhaps you have family or other obligations that limit your options. It is still possible that you might find real love with someone who is willing to share these burdens with you. And it is possible that, even if none of these burdens are yours, you might find real love with someone who is thus affected.

Real love is actually much easier to find than perfect love. The fantasy of perfect love is focused exclusively on one person, that perfect partner with whom all your desires for intimacy and love will finally be fulfilled. A person who is looking for perfect love can be disinclined to develop any meaningful friendships with anyone he or she does not view as a marriage prospect. Friendships with single persons of the opposite sex can seem dangerous (what if you fall into sin?), and friendships with anyone else can seem beside the point (since romance is presumed to be by definition the only source of intimacy). It is no wonder that single people who take this approach to life and relationships are lonely.

Real love, on the other hand, can be found in differing depths and intensities, and sometimes in seemingly unlikely places. Real love values friendship with people who are like you and people who are unlike you, with people who are already members of your family (parents and grandparents, brothers and sisters, aunts and uncles and cousins) and people who are unlikely ever to be members of your family (friends, neighbors, schoolmates, coworkers, little old ladies from church). Invite any person in any of these

categories out for lunch, ask a few questions, listen attentively and
see if you don't find your life enriched.

Real love allows you to be honest about your desire to find a
marriage partner. "I detest when people say that after they got
their priorities in order and truly 'gave dating and finding a mate
up to God,' then God provided a soul mate," wrote one woman. "It
puts terrible guilt and pressure on a single person who is not in a
relationship: not only must there be something physically wrong
with them to turn off members of the opposite sex, but something
must be spiritually wrong too."

It is hard enough to navigate feelings about so complex a thing
as marriage without having your relationship status turned into a
magnifying glass trained on your spiritual condition. And it is
hard enough to wait for a relationship you deeply desire without
being made to feel that you will only get what you want if you can
persuade yourself and God that you can be happy without it. Living with longing and uncertainty is part of what it means to be a
human being. Real love allows you to tell the truth about what you
want and what your feelings are.

Real love allows for the possibility that not every dating relationship should lead to marriage. "I've heard people say that God
wouldn't allow them to love one another if he didn't mean for them
to be together," wrote one man. But it is easy to fall in love with
someone who for one reason or other is not a wise choice. The
mere fact that you love someone is not evidence either that this is
God's chosen mate for you, or that you would do well to marry
him or her.

The fantasy of perfect love, by contrast, assumes that you are
dating this person precisely because you believe he or she is God's
choice for you. Every relational difficulty thus becomes a test of
faith: God brought you together, God wants you to stay together,
and so the only faithful thing to do is to stay in the relationship

and work on it. People spend months and years in relationships that are going from bad to worse, because it just doesn't seem Christian to call it quits. Real love does not require that you do this. Real love is compatible with wisdom and prudence.

Real love in fact requires that you act wisely. "I was reading books that told me, 'Follow Jesus, pray for your husband, and God will give you the man of your dreams,'" wrote another woman. "So I went looking and praying, and when a boy came along I grabbed him." Unfortunately, she did not notice a number of red flags until it was too late and she had been badly hurt. Trusting God does not negate the need to use your own good judgment.

Real love has room for the good judgment of others as well. There are, one hopes, a number of people in your life who want the best for you, whose judgment is sound and whose lives will be affected by the choices you make. Your decisions about love and marriage are not just about you; they are elements of a larger network of relationships of which you are already a part. You are likely to be able to make better decisions if you seek out conversation with others about these things.

Not everyone's advice is equally good. Some parents, for example, are truly wise, and their children do well to take their opinions very seriously. Other parents are for one reason or another not so able to guide their children well. If this is the case with your parents, you need to listen for other, wiser voices, trusting that you will be able to find good conversation partners who can help you come to a nuanced and honest evaluation of your relationship and of your options.

Real love gives you the freedom to consider your own feelings and desires. Do you wish to marry a given person, or not? It can be easy to conflate a desire for marriage in general with a desire to marry a particular person. If you have always wanted to be married, or you are approaching a time in your life when it seems that you ought to be getting married, you may suppose that any person who is willing to marry you is the right person for you. It can likewise be easy to fear that if you don't marry this person now, you will never have another chance.

It is true that you cannot know what other opportunities for marriage you may ever have. For this reason, any decision not to marry a particular person is a decision to remain single, at least for now, and maybe forever. But while there may have been times and places in which any marriage was better than no marriage, this is not the case in contemporary American society. If you have to make it on your own, you can. Real love frees you to do your best to make a good decision about this person and this relationship, and to leave your future in God's hands, where it belongs.

The Good News

Martin Luther draws a contrast between what he calls a theology of glory and a theology of the cross. A theology of glory finds God in sunsets and cathedrals and anywhere else that seems magnificent and triumphant. A theology of the cross finds God in a cradle in Bethlehem, in a garden at Gethsemane, on a cross outside the walls of Jerusalem. A theology of the cross, in other words, finds God not as we might imagine or desire him to be, but as he actually is, taking upon himself the frailties and sorrows of humanity and transforming them by the mysterious power of his death and resurrection.

Too many of the judgments about marriage found in Christian romantic advice books are, in essence, theologies of glory. While the authors of these books may say that they believe in marriage "for better or for worse," in actual practice they promise bliss, pure bliss, if only we will follow their advice about finding romance with the perfect partner who, they assure us, is part of God's plan for us. A Christian romance, a Christian wedding, a Christian marriage—all are presumed to be provinces of all the perfection that a heart formed by Hollywood could possibly desire.

But the hearts of Christians are supposed to be formed by the gospel. The gospel is a success story, but it is a paradoxical success. When Jesus, the king of glory, rides into Jerusalem, he does so on a donkey. When Jesus invites his hearers to share in his life, he does so by inviting them into his death: "If any [one] would come after me, let him deny himself and take up his cross and follow me" (Matthew 16:24). And when Jesus reconciles the world to God, he does so by himself entering into the very abyss of alienation: "My God, my God, why hast thou forsaken me?" (Matthew 27:46).

Genuinely faithful accounts of the Christian life and of Christian relationships have at their center these and other paradoxes characteristic of the gospel. Marriage is a good gift of God. It can be a powerful presence for good in the lives of marital partners, of their children, and of the broader communities of which they are a part. But marriage is for better and for worse, for richer and for poorer, in sickness and in health. A person is not guaranteed bliss if he or she marries, or guaranteed woe if he or she doesn't. Marriage is one possible path in life. As such, it participates in all the shadows and sorrows of life, and at the same time can be shaped from within by the paradoxical and redeeming love of God.

The good news is that Christian marriage is possible. It is possible for Christians to choose one another wisely, love one another well, welcome children joyfully, live together faithfully, and look back together with pleasure and thanksgiving on the life that has been theirs. The good news is that even in the midst of the very real challenges and limitations and sorrows of real life, real people can find real love.

2

Marriage

What Makes It Christian?

I T'S HARD TO KNOW WHAT TO THINK about marriage these days. On the one hand, marriage seems omnipresent, an institution so deep-rooted and widespread that it is hard to imagine the world without it. People grow up; they get married. Christians especially get married—it's a Christian thing to do. They get married for sex, they get married for children, they get married so they won't be alone. They get married because they're tired of being asked at every family reunion they attend, "So—when are you getting married?"

On the other hand, marriage seems ever more marginalized, as the world appears to move inexorably in other directions. Increasing numbers of people spend increasing proportions of their lives as single persons: they marry later, they divorce more frequently, and they are far more likely to live with an intimate companion without being married to him or her than were members of previous generations. In 1930, 84 percent of American households were headed by married couples; in 2006, fewer than half were.[1]

And marriage can seem not only imperiled but perilous. Mar-

---

[1]Sam Roberts, "To Be Married Means to Be Outnumbered," *New York Times*, October 15, 2006.

riages go bad, and people get hurt. Husbands and wives end up angry and resentful, exhausted and lonely, abusive or battered. "When I look at my parents, I wonder what is keeping them together," says one young woman. "If this is what marriage is, I don't want it." Like many other children of empty or conflict-ridden marriages, she wonders whether divorce would be preferable to married misery.

Too easily, marriage can come to seem simultaneously like an impossible dream and an inevitable nightmare. We long for marriage, and we are terrified of it. We are afraid we will fail as our parents failed before us. We are afraid we will be betrayed. We are afraid we will be miserable, that we will be not loved but enslaved, that things will get bad and we will just have to live with it. Marriage can come to seem like an undertaking in which some make it and some don't, and we fear we will be among those who don't.

And yet, we want to be married. We want to find the courage to try and the secret to success. But what is it? The advice many Christian young people seem most often to be given is that they must keep God at the center of their relationships. They take this advice to heart; every time we teach our marriage class, we hear more students telling us that they want to keep God at the center of their relationships. "What does that mean?" we ask them. Mostly they're not sure.

Our sense is that this phrase expresses a desire for a marriage that is distinctively Christian and thus secure against failure. But even putting it that way leaves a lot of blanks to be filled in. What exactly is a Christian marriage, and what makes it secure? Is a Christian marriage one in which both the bride and the groom are virgins until they wed? Is a Christian marriage one in which both parties firmly resolve before marriage that they will never consider divorce?

If husbands and wives read the Bible and pray together, is their marriage Christian? If they just go to church together, is that good enough? Must Christian spouses have children? Must they rear their children in particular ways? Must they hold particular views on gender roles, or divide up household responsibilities in particular ways? How are spouses in a Christian marriage supposed to handle conflict? Is conflict even allowed in a Christian marriage? Or is conflict a sub-Christian indication that God is not, in fact, at the center of this relationship?

In this chapter we will turn to Christian Scripture and tradition for the beginnings of answers to some of these questions. What is Christian marriage? What is it not? And how can Christians find ways in the midst of contemporary culture to counter marital failure and foster success in marriage?

What Marriage Is

Marriage is not a Christian monopoly. People get married because they are human, not just because they are Christian. And Christians themselves have not always gotten married in distinctively Christian ways. In the early centuries of the church, most Christians married in small ceremonies at home that were arranged by their families and shaped by local law and custom. Beginning in the fifth century, clergy who married were required to have their marriages blessed in church, and it appears that some—but by no means all—lay Christians also sought priestly blessing for their marriages.[2]

In the eleventh and twelfth centuries, the requirement that Christian marriages be celebrated in church was extended to all persons. In actual practice, this requirement affected mostly per-

---

[2]Mark Searle and Kenneth W. Stevenson, *Documents of the Marriage Liturgy* (Collegeville, Minn.: Liturgical, 1992), pp. 253-55. The requirement that clergy marry in church obviously predates the later requirement in the Western church that clergy remain celibate.

sons of property and power, who needed the official blessing of the church on their marriages so they could pass on their property to their legitimate heirs. People of the lower classes, with little or no property to leave to anyone, had no need for legitimate heirs and in many cases continued with older practices such as marriage by consent (that is, by declaring in the presence of two witnesses that they took each other as husband and wife), by a private promise to marry followed by sexual relations, or simply by living together and presenting themselves as husband and wife, the legal presumption being that if they did so, they must at some point have exchanged consent.[3]

Both the Catholic hierarchy and, eventually, the Protestant Reformers took a dim view of such "irregular" marriages, in part because they allowed young people to marry without the consent (or even knowledge) of their parents, and in part because they lent themselves to the victimization of vulnerable girls by unscrupulous suitors who could seduce them with promises of marriage and deny in the morning that any such promise had ever been made. Among Protestants this desire to reform abuses in marital practice was joined with a renewed vision for marriage itself. Where the medieval Catholic church had seen marriage as the second-best path in life (the best path being the celibate life of the monk, nun or priest), sixteenth-century Protestants saw marriage as among God's most fundamental designs for human life, and thus as the preferred path in life for the vast majority of people.

Protestant convictions about marriage are reflected in the marriage liturgies written by a variety of Reformation-era pastors for use among their congregants. In the English-speaking world the best-known such liturgy is by Thomas Cranmer, which appeared

---

[3]Brian Dempsey, "Farewell Then Common Law Marriage," *Journal of the Law Society of Scotland,* December 12, 2005 <www.journalonline.co.uk/Magazine/50-12/1002528.aspx>.

in its earliest version in the first Book of Common Prayer in 1549 and has remained mostly intact through many subsequent revisions of the prayer book.[4] This is the source of the familiar words, "Dearly beloved friends, we are gathered together here in the sight of God, and in the face of his congregation, to join together this Man and this Woman in holy Matrimony . . ." For nearly five hundred years, all over the world and in the marriages of countless millions of couples, these words and the liturgy that they introduce have expressed Christian convictions about what marriage is and what Christian couples should be hoping and striving for in their own marriages.

So what is marriage? To begin with, says Cranmer, marriage is "an honorable estate." God instituted marriage in paradise before the fall. It is not a human invention, and it was not originally a response to sin. Marriage is a reflection or an image of God's relationship with human beings. Jesus Christ serves as the mediator of that relationship, and marriage is thus a sign of the union of Christ with the church. Catholics had understood (and still do understand) the marriage of baptized Christians as a sacrament. For Protestants, marriage is not officially a sacrament, but it retains a sacramental function. Marriage points beyond itself to a greater union, and itself participates in a mysterious and real way in that union.

Because marriage is God's own creation, it follows that humans do well to enter into marriage for reasons that are congruent with God's designs for marriage. People are all too inclined to twist created things to their own ends, proceeding not by enlightened reason but rather by (fallen) human instinct, "like brute beasts that have no understanding," in Cranmer's memorable phrase. This is

---

[4]The Book of Common Prayer is available in many published versions and also online. For the 1549 text see, for example, Henry Baskerville Walton, ed., *The First Book of Common Prayer of Edward VI* (London: Rivingtons, 1870).

not a good idea. We must enter into marriage "reverently, discreetly, advisedly, soberly, and in the fear of God, duly considering the causes for the which Matrimony was ordained."

Cranmer names the first of these causes as the procreation of children. Nowadays this strikes a lot of people as a weirdly distorted view of marriage, as if something peripheral has by mistake been placed in the foreground. Most of the young people we know want children, eventually, but virtually all of them embark upon marriage, or plan to embark upon marriage, with a firm intention not to have children "yet." They marry (or plan to marry) for sex, for companionship, for love; the prospect of children is only the tiniest cloud on their horizon.

Openness to marriage but not (yet) to children is only possible in a society where contraception is readily available. Only then can children be seen as an option or an extra, the understanding being that married couples are free to choose when to have children, and how many to have, and whether to have them at all. In fact, this vision is often an illusion. Married couples routinely conceive children that they hadn't "meant" to have.[5] When a couple has not actively been hoping for a child, news of a pregnancy is sometimes met with astonishment or dismay—this is not at all what this husband and wife had in mind. But how is it possible to enter into the sexual partnership that is marriage, and then be dismayed by pregnancy? What do we think marriage is for?

Of course it is not only the married who experience "unplanned" pregnancies. It used to be that unmarried couples who conceived were pressured to marry. Nowadays, such couples are more often pressured not to marry, on the assumption that if you

---

[5] An estimated 30 percent of pregnancies among married women are unintended at the time of conception. See Stanley K. Henshaw, "Unintended Pregnancy in the United States," *Family Planning Perspectives* 30, no. 1 (January/February 1998): 24-29, 46.

get married because you "have to," you will necessarily end up miserable or divorced. Of course, some unmarried persons choose as sexual partners people who would not be suitable marriage partners. When a child is conceived in the context of such a relationship, often there are better options than the marriage of the expectant mother and father.

But where expectant parents are decent people who are reasonably well suited to each other, the desire to legitimize a pregnancy can be a very good reason to get married, precisely because that is one of the things that marriage is for: to create a family in which you can welcome and raise children. Such an understanding of marriage is fundamentally at odds with modern romantic notions of marriage as an essentially private relationship between two adults. But in a traditionally Christian understanding, while marriage is a freely chosen bond between two adults, the resulting community is one of hospitality, and the children born of that union are its most honored guests.

The second cause for which God ordained marriage, says Cranmer, is "for a remedy against sin and to avoid fornication, that such persons as have not the gift of continence might marry." This sounds very old-fashioned and censorious. But when Cranmer wrote these words, these were new ideas, and grace-filled ones. The pastors and theologians of the patristic and medieval eras displayed, in many cases, distinctly negative views of both sex and marriage. These negative attitudes played into the growing exaltation of virginity over marriage, and into the extension of the celibate ethic to include all clergy, parish priests as well as cloistered monks and nuns.

By the later middle ages, that celibate ethic was in disarray. Many parish priests found themselves unable to keep their vows of celibacy, and lived instead in sexual relationships with mistresses who were the mothers of their illegitimate children but who had no legal standing and no rights of inheritance. The Protestant Reformation, with its rethinking of the moral status of celibacy and marriage, was attractive to many of these clergy precisely because it offered them a way to make honorable wives of their mistresses and legitimate children of their offspring.

In such a context, it is a positive thing to call marriage a "remedy against sin." In the Middle Ages, all sex, even married sex, was seen as morally dubious, and the only real remedy against sexual sin was understood to be celibacy. This left those who were unable to remain celibate but forbidden to marry in a moral quandary. But as the Protestants saw it, matrimony was God's good gift to all—including clergy—who did not have the "gift of continence," which in this context meant the ability to keep a vow of celibacy.

In our day, the questions and challenges are different, but the solution may well be the same. The freedom promised by the sexual revolution has come to look in many instances more like bondage: bondage to fear, to disease, to unwanted pregnancy, to abortion, to the numbing of soul and body that seems so often to be the effect of indiscriminately scattered sexual behavior. Perhaps what we need is an anchor in the storm, a way to channel and direct our sexual energies in a way that establishes and builds up—rather than undermining and destroying—our own self-in-relationship as well as that of our partner. Perhaps what we need is marriage.

The third cause for marriage, according to Cranmer, is "the mutual society, help, and comfort, that the one ought to have of the other, both in prosperity and adversity." Human beings are made for community. They were created male and female in the image of God, who as Holy Trinity exists from everlasting to everlasting as the divine community of Father, Son and Holy Spirit. Marriage is that mode of human community that, in a Christian understanding, most closely reflects God's own being-in-community.

This aspect of marriage is the one most clearly in view at the beginning of Christian Scripture. In Genesis 2, God creates Eve from Adam's side and presents her to him. Adam responds, "This at last is bone of my bones and flesh of my flesh; she shall be called Woman, because she was taken out of Man." The author of Genesis continues, "Therefore a man leaves his father and his mother and cleaves to his wife, and they become one flesh" (Genesis 2:23-24). The created differentiation of humans into male and female finds its completion and its goal in the union of husband and wife in marriage.

This companionate aspect of marriage tends to be the most immediately attractive one to many modern persons, but with a caveat. The ideal relationship, we are taught to think, is one in which the partners could each manage perfectly well independently of one another, but choose for the sake of personal fulfillment to do things together instead. "Mutual society" thus sounds good; "help and comfort" sound less good. You don't want to be trapped, after all, in a situation in which you are dependent on someone else or someone else is dependent on you.

In truth, of course, human beings don't just enjoy one another's company; we need each other. There are seasons in everyone's life in which his or her primary posture is one of dependence: childhood, old age, illness and disability come immediately to mind. And dependence and interdependence are threads that are woven through the lives even of those who happen at the moment to be healthy, able-bodied and in the prime of life.

Marriage is thus a school for character. But it is not the only school for character. Human beings are called to learn to love and care for one another whether or not they are married. But marriage is at least this: an arena in which we can practice the art of faithfully bearing with one another in the midst of all that life brings. It is an opportunity for mutual society, help and comfort, both in prosperity and adversity.

What Marriage Is Not

Christians have over the years reflected not only on what marriage is, but on what it is not. A prominent theme in early Christian thinking about marriage is that marriage is not obligatory. In contrast to the prevailing Jewish view that obedience to the divine command to "be fruitful and multiply" made marriage and parenthood a religious duty in all but the rarest of cases, Paul suggests in 1 Corinthians 7 that singleness may in fact be preferable to marriage. Marriage is a good thing, says Paul, and it has its place, but "in view of the present distress"—by which Paul probably meant the imminent return of Christ—it is better for unmarried persons to remain single (1 Corinthians 7:26). Married people are anxious about the well-being of their spouses; unmarried people are able, by contrast, to give their full attention to spiritual affairs. Thus "he who marries his betrothed does well; and he who refrains from marriage will do better" (1 Corinthians 7:38).

For this and other reasons, Christians eventually came to esteem virginity over marriage. They understood matrimony as a good way to be obedient to God; but celibacy, they thought, was a better way to be holy. Celibacy was not mere singleness—it was a vowed state akin to matrimony, only in this case the vow was not a vow of marriage but a vow of perpetual virginity for the sake of the kingdom of God.[6] The celibate ethic developed gradually, beginning with groups of virgins and widows who lived in community and devoted themselves to works of mercy, and extending to hermits, monks living in cloisters, and eventually, in the Western

---

[6]A key biblical passage adduced in support of this view is this story told about Jesus in the Gospel of Matthew: "The disciples said to [Jesus], 'If such is the case of a man with his wife, it is not expedient to marry.' But he said to them, 'Not all men can receive this saying, but only those to whom it is given. For there are eunuchs who have been so from birth, and there are eunuchs who have been made eunuchs by men, and there are eunuchs who have made themselves eunuchs for the sake of the kingdom of heaven. He who is able to receive this, let him receive it'" (Matthew 19:10-12).

church, to all ordained clergy. By the late middle ages, due to the large numbers of people in religious life and the bars to lawful marriage that existed for people in certain social and economic situations, the majority of Europeans were either celibate or simply unmarried.[7]

This all changed dramatically in the sixteenth century, at least in those parts of Europe that were touched by the Protestant Reformation. Protestants dismantled the theological framework that had supported celibacy, arguing that the ability to keep a vow of perpetual virginity was a gift given to a few, not a law that the church could or should impose on the many. Matrimony, not celibacy, was the normal vocation of most people. In territories newly converted to the Reformation, the doors of cloisters were opened, and all monks or nuns who wished to marry were granted the freedom to do so. Many did so desire, and for a couple of generations they mostly married each other. Many former nuns also married former priests. These newly formed clerical families were the prototypes of a new social and ecclesial order: the Protestant pastor and his family.[8]

In our day there is a curiously mixed state of affairs, in which among Protestants at least it is assumed that the normal way to be an adult Christian is to be married, and yet increasing numbers of Christian adults are in fact single. Marriage is virtually universal among Protestant pastors. Most positions of influence and power in most churches are occupied by married persons. But marriage is becoming less and less common among church members: the

---

[7]Steven Ozment, *Ancestors: The Loving Family in Old Europe* (Cambridge, Mass.: Harvard University Press, 2001), p. 33. This is not so great a contrast to the present day: while celibacy is no longer common, singleness is increasingly so. According to recent census data, nearly half (46 percent) of all Americans over age eighteen are either unmarried or living apart from a spouse (Sam Roberts, "Census Finds Fewer Homes Have a Child in Residence," *New York Times*, February 26, 2009).

[8]David C. Steinmetz, "Luther and Formation in Faith," in *Luther in Context*, 2nd ed. (Grand Rapids: Baker Academic, 2002), pp. 131-32.

widowed, the divorced and the never-married account for significant numbers of persons in the pew. But where is the theological and practical support for their single state? Too often there isn't any. Instead there is a singles' group in which, it is hoped, unattached persons will find each other, pair off, and become the way Christian people are supposed to be—married.

This is not good enough. The Christian church has never made marriage a law. Christians have always had the freedom not to marry, and thus freedom to serve God in either the married or the single state. But the freedom to remain single is seriously compromised when there appears to be no recognition within the church that singleness is a normal condition for an adult. And the freedom to marry is compromised, too, when marriage is seen not as a possibility but as a necessity, at least if one hopes ever to be integrated into the center of the life of the church. There is a real need in the church for a more nuanced and developed theology of singleness, along with practical efforts to create opportunities for meaningful life and relationship for people apart from marriage. These can only be good for everyone, whether married or single.

Another thing Christians have come to believe about marriage is that marriage is not disembodied. Marriage is not an ethereal relationship between souls; it is a physical relationship between embodied persons. Brides and grooms give themselves to one another in marriage, and thereafter the husband's body belongs not to himself but to his wife, and the wife's body belongs not to herself but to her husband (1 Corinthians 7:3-5). This gift of the body does not convey a right to abuse or domineer over the spouse; on the contrary, it becomes an invitation to self-giving love. Husbands are to love their wives as they love their own bodies, nourishing and cherishing them even as Christ nourishes and cherishes the church (Ephesians 5:28-29).

The mutual gift of spouses' bodies to each other gives sex a special status within marriage, and adultery a special status among sins. Sexual relations are not incidental to marriage but intrinsic to it. Nonconsummation is grounds for annulment (that is, a determination that there is in fact no marriage), and the long-term, unreasonable refusal of sexual relations in a previously consummated marriage is seen by some Christian communions as grounds for divorce. And sexual relations with anyone other than the spouse constitutes a profound betrayal, not because there are no other ways to hurt one's husband or wife deeply, but because adultery strikes at the very heart of the marital relationship, taking a body that properly belongs to the spouse and giving it to another, and thus at the same time introducing a third party into a marriage bed that is properly reserved for husband and wife alone.

The embodied nature of marriage is also why until very recently it was universally assumed that marriage is necessarily a bond between a man and a woman. In a Christian understanding, the premise of marriage is God's creation of humans as male and female. People do not exist in the world as androgynous, disembodied souls; they exist as men or as women. And yet there are not two human races, one male and one female; humanity is male and female, together. Individual marriages are particular expressions of this deep unity of the human race, as one man and one woman leave their parents and cleave to one another, becoming one flesh.

Thus while children are the natural—one might even say normal—result of the marital union, procreation is not intrinsic to marriage in the way that the union of a man and a woman is intrinsic to marriage. Not every couple is blessed with children. Some couples go into marriage either suspecting or knowing full well that they will not be blessed with children. And yet such couples are truly married, because marriage consists not in childbearing but in the joining of husband and wife in this embodied covenant.

A third thing that Christians have come of necessity to realize about marriage is that it is not foolproof. Just because people make wedding vows does not mean they will keep them. Marital failure has been part of the landscape of marriage ever since Eve shared the apple with Adam and he blamed her for the fact that he took it. Divorce, however, took longer to arrive on the scene. The first mentions of divorce in Christian Scripture are in the book of Deuteronomy, where it is assumed that divorce occurs and an effort is made to regulate some of the circumstances surrounding it.[9] Thereafter the images of marriage and divorce, and fidelity and adultery, are among the most common metaphors invoked in Scripture to characterize the relationship of God to his people and the nature and consequences of Israel's betrayal of that relationship.[10]

In the New Testament the treatment of divorce is both brief and not entirely univocal. In the Gospels of Mark and Luke, Jesus states that remarriage after any divorce amounts to adultery (Mark 10:2-12; Luke 16:16-18), and in the Gospel of Matthew, he makes an exception for divorce on the grounds of "unchastity" (Matthew 5:31-32; 19:3-9). Paul discusses divorce briefly in 1 Corinthians, suggesting that a believer married to an unbelieving spouse is not obliged to divorce, but may do so if the unbelieving spouse desires it (1 Corinthians 7:10-16). The overall impression given is that Jesus and the authors of Scripture are less interested in issuing specific rules and regulations to govern divorce, than they are in underscoring the nature of marriage itself as a holy and transforming covenant meant to mirror God's loving and faithful relationship with God's people.[11]

---

[9]Deuteronomy 24:1-4 requires a man who divorces his wife to give her a certificate of divorce (a document of legal protection that would prove that she was free to remarry) and prohibits that man from remarrying his divorced wife. The act of divorcing itself is not given legal status in Deuteronomy; it is simply assumed.

[10]See, for example, Jeremiah 3:6-10; Hosea 1:1–2:23; Malachi 2:13-16.

[11]For a summary of recent scholarship on this subject, see Richard B. Hays, *The Moral*

In the early centuries of the church, Jesus' emphasis on the intended permanence of marriage led Christians to conclude that Christian marriage was in its very nature indissoluble; God had made it this way, and no amount of human failure could change the fact that a husband and wife were bound to each other for as long as they both lived. If conditions within a marriage became truly intolerable, husbands and wives could petition to be relieved of the ordinary duty of married couples to live together and sleep together—that is, they could ask for and be granted a "separation from bed and board." But they were still legally married, and neither of them was free to marry anyone else as long as the other lived.[12]

It was also possible that what looked like a marriage might be found by a church court to be not really a marriage after all. A couple might be found to have violated one of the many rules that regulated who was eligible to marry whom—rules about how closely related people could be, or how old they had to be, for example. Or it might be found that one or both of the spouses was coerced into the marriage or never intended to fulfill his or her marriage vows. In cases like these the marriage could be annulled. This did not mean the parties were now divorced; rather, it meant that they had never been married at all and were now free to marry as any unmarried person is free to marry.

These were among the regulations that changed among Protestants beginning in the sixteenth century. The Protestant Reformers vastly simplified what had become an enormously complex system of canon law related to matrimony, reducing to a minimum the thicket of regulations that had grown over the course of the Middle Ages. And for the first time in a long time they articu-

Vision of the New Testament (San Francisco: HarperSanFrancisco, 1996), pp. 347-78.
[12]Steven Ozment, *When Fathers Ruled: Family Life in Reformation Europe* (Cambridge, Mass.: Harvard University Press, 1983), p. 87.

lated the conviction that there could actually be such a thing as divorce. In certain situations a Christian marriage could be dissolved, leaving at least one of the parties free to remarry even during the former spouse's lifetime.

The circumstances identified by the Protestant Reformers as possible grounds for divorce were limited: an inability to consummate the marriage, adultery, life-threatening violence, a refusal to engage in sexual relations with the spouse, a refusal to live with the spouse.[13] The willingness of the Reformers actually to countenance divorce even on legitimate grounds was limited as well. Martin Luther, for example, advised more than one unhappily married spouse to enter into a secret (and bigamous) second marriage rather than openly to divorce his or her first spouse.[14] But the Protestant affirmation that it was possible for a marriage truly to exist and then truly to be dissolved, combined with the decision to move the adjudication of marriage and divorce cases from the ecclesiastical to the civil courts, opened the door to the possibility of civil divorce as it exists today.

The advent of no-fault divorce law in the twentieth century changed the nature of the game again. Until then any person who wanted a divorce had to claim that the other party was at fault, with the relevant faults being more or less identical with the possible grounds for divorce recognized among Protestants since the sixteenth century. If the other party contested the divorce, it could easily become financially or logistically impossible to prove fault in court, particularly for women, who tended to have less access to marital property (like money) and to be more likely to be victims of abuse than men. No-fault divorce was introduced in an attempt

---

[13]Steven Ozment, *Protestants: The Birth of a Revolution* (New York: Doubleday, 1992), p. 163.

[14]"Luther preferred such an arrangement to outright divorce because he believed it ensured continuing companionship and support for each spouse . . . while at the same time it prevented whoring and adultery." Ibid.

to lessen the damage done to women, children and families as a whole by the previous fault-based system of divorce.

We all know what happened next. Once divorces were available for the asking, divorce rates skyrocketed, doubling in the thirty years between 1950 and 1980.[15] Although divorce rates have declined somewhat since then, it is still estimated that around 45 percent of first marriages will end in divorce, with rates significantly higher for second and third marriages. And whole armies of sociologists and psychologists have built careers documenting and lamenting the damage that the fragmenting of the family is doing to men, women and—especially—children. Clearly, there has to be more to marriage than simply getting married. Marriage is not foolproof; by themselves wedding vows do not accomplish or fix much of anything.

Thinking About Divorce

What can Christians do to foster success in marriage? One thing they can do is think hard about divorce—why marriages end in divorce, what strategies individual Christians and church communities might put in place to counter divorce, and how individuals and churches might respond to divorce when it does occur. This might seem counterintuitive. If your intention is to support marriage, wouldn't it make more sense not to think about divorce? Wouldn't it make more sense to say, "Divorce is not an option," and leave it at that?

The reality is that divorce is not just an "option" that smart and moral people can decide ahead of time to choose or not to

---

[15]The divorce rate in 1950 was 2.6 divorces per 1000 population; in 1980 the divorce rate was 5.2 divorces per 1000 population. The rate remained steady at around 5 divorces per 1000 population for about five years and declined slowly thereafter; in 2001 the rate was 4 divorces per 1000 population. See the 2003 Statistical Abstract of the U.S., Section 2, Table 83, p. 4, at <www.census.gov/prod/2004pubs/03statab/vitstat.pdf>.

choose, with the result being that the only people who remain at risk of divorce are the weak-willed and the clueless. In fact, "divorce is not an option" can be code for "since I know I will never get a divorce, I don't have to worry about the possible outcomes of any problems that might develop in my marriage." Then, since ignoring problems can be more comfortable than facing them and dealing with them, the problems that do develop get ignored and pushed aside and left to fester until they erupt in a gigantic mess that it is too late to do anything about, and divorce starts to look like the least bad of the available options—even to people who at some earlier date might truly have believed that "divorce is not an option."

So why do people divorce? Do they marry the wrong person, and thus doom themselves from the beginning? Are they too lazy or weak to muscle through the difficulties that inevitably come with marriage? Are they tempted to take the "easy way out" by lax civil law concerning divorce, or by lax moral standards within the church? Each of these possibilities suggests a solution. If people divorce because they marry the wrong person, then a good initial choice is a key to avoiding divorce. If people divorce because they aren't willing to stick with marriage when things get hard, then a greater degree of commitment to marriage is required. If lax civil law is the problem, then laws that protect marriages and children are needed. If the church is not supporting marriage, then it needs to do so.

There is a grain of truth in each of these suggestions. Making a good choice of a partner is a crucial element in building a strong marriage. But a good initial choice is not the end of the matter. Life is full of choices, and lots of them come after the wedding. When you choose a spouse, you choose a partner with whom to begin a journey. Much of the subsequent health and success of your partnership will hinge on choices you make together over the course of that journey. When a marriage ends in divorce, sometimes it does so not because the initial choice was bad, but because too many of the subsequent choices pushed the couple apart rather than drawing them together.

Commitment is an important factor in being able to make the kinds of choices that can draw you and your spouse closer together over a lifetime. What is needed, though, is not commitment to marriage itself in some abstract, teeth-gritted sense, but a living commitment to your spouse in particular and to the marriage that is your joint project. Abstract commitments don't keep people married; too often, they just make people feel trapped. An active commitment to this person and this marriage, expressed in ongoing cooperative efforts to build a common life, is far more likely to result in a partnership whose roots are deep enough to sustain you both through good and bad times.

Civil law and other social policies do affect all of us to a greater degree than we may be consciously aware of. It is possible, however, that marriages are affected less by marital law per se than by laws and policies that affect the conditions in which couples and families live. Do zoning laws encourage the existence of neighborhoods in which individuals and families can live in supportive community with one another? Are adequate housing, health care and child care accessible and affordable to all families? The greater the degree of mutuality and support that characterizes a given couple's circumstances, the greater the likelihood is that that couple will be able to build a strong and enduring marriage. And the reverse is also true: given enough isolation and economic and other strain, just about any marriage is liable to collapse.

And church communities certainly affect the health and strength of the marriages within them. But do churches actually support marriage and specific married persons? Or do they discourage and stigmatize divorce and divorced persons, and suppose that somehow this equals support for marriage? Too often it seems that the latter strategy is the one actually implemented. One way this is frequently attempted is through the limitation of acceptable grounds for divorce. Where the Protestant Reformers identified a number of such grounds, including abandonment and abuse, some modern Protestants see only one: adultery. As one person wrote: "I have always been taught that adultery is the only biblical reason to get a divorce."

The appeal of such an understanding is that it seems to bring clarity to the murkiness of marital discord. Has adultery been committed? Then divorce is permissible. Has adultery not been committed? Then divorce is not permissible; the problems must be "worked out" and the marriage "saved." It also seems to bring clarity to the murkiness of church discipline. If a couple divorces, the task of the church is to identify the adulterer (if there is one). That person is the guilty party, and the offended spouse is the innocent party; the church can then blame the guilty party, "forgive" the innocent party (who doesn't actually need forgiveness because he or she is not guilty), and feel satisfied that it has thus positioned itself as a champion of marriage.[16]

This isn't even good in theory, and in practice it is a disaster. Attempts to make black-and-white judgments about the justifiability of divorce on the basis of narrow and rigid criteria too often founder on the messy shoals of reality. Just how adulterous does an adulterer have to be before his or her adultery "counts"? Is any sex act good enough, or does it have to be a particular one? And what if the assault on the marriage vows is not sexual but is of some other

---

[16]For a scholarly treatment of divorce that takes the view that in any divorce, there is a maximum of one possible "innocent" party (i.e., a spouse who neither committed adultery nor sought a divorce for any illegitimate reason) and that the right to remarry belongs only to such innocent parties, see, e.g., Craig Keener, *And Marries Another: Divorce and Remarriage in the Teaching of the New Testament* (Peabody, Mass.: Hendrickson, 1991), pp. 48-49, 65-66 and passim.

nature? Must a Christian spouse submit to violence or other forms of abuse, as long as the other spouse is not adulterous?

In addition, the identification of guilty and innocent parties, the blaming and shaming of the guilty and the exoneration of the innocent, is at the same time simplistic and not in accordance with the substance of the gospel. It is simplistic in the sense that very few divorces involve completely innocent parties. Just as it takes two to tango, it takes two to make a relationship that ends in failure and divorce. Where infidelity ends a marriage, there are usually other problems as well, problems to which both spouses have contributed and for which they both need to accept responsibility. In such circumstances, to focus exclusively on the guilty party's offense is to hand the innocent party a kind of "get out of jail free" card: "Your spouse committed adultery? Well, you're off the hook—so glad to hear it wasn't your fault."

This is not only unseemly; it isn't even Christian. In a Christian understanding, there is none that is righteous—no, not one—and the offer of forgiveness and grace is made to all. This goes for divorce as well as for anything else. Forgiveness and second chances are not reserved for innocent people who don't need them. They are God's offer to guilty people, and that is all of us. Marital failure is like any other kind of failure—it is serious, it has consequences that none of us would prefer to live with, and it is a circumstance in which we can receive God's renewing grace.

It is sadly worth noting how often churches and individuals end up identifying women as the guilty parties in divorce. The "get out of jail free" excuse for nonadulterous spouses tends only to come into play when it is the wife who is the adulterer. When a husband is unfaithful, a good Christian wife is expected to stand by her man, because after all, divorce is not an option. If she divorces him anyway, she thereby becomes the guilty party herself: she has failed to save the marriage, which is her responsibility as a Christian wife. The husband is received sympathetically into the bosom of the church, which is eager to show him the forgiveness his wife has failed to offer him, and the wife is hounded out of the church, because God hates divorce.

It grieves us to have to describe the behavior of the Christian church this way, but in too many cases it is sadly true. It is true in seemingly clear-cut cases involving adultery, and it is even more often true in cases in which the problems in the marriage are of some other kind: alcoholism, chronic deception, addiction to pornography, irresponsibility with money, mistreatment of the children or of the spouse. The results are devastating. One young man described to us the circumstances of his parents' divorce: his father, an abusive alcoholic, kicked his mother out. The church blamed her—she had failed to stand by him and make the marriage work. "I HATE THIS!" the son wrote. "Why should my mother be afraid to go to church, or cry after going? Are Christians not supposed to learn from Christ himself? Did he reject anyone? Give belittling eyes? I do not think so."

This is not support for marriage. It does nothing to strengthen existing marriages, or to heal men and women and children who have been wounded by marital failure and divorce. The church can and must do better. If church communities and individual Christians were willing to suffer with those affected by divorce, they might develop an empathy and compassion that could assist them in supporting couples through the stresses and strains of married life and toward the satisfaction and confidence that come with meeting such challenges well.

Love Without Fear

"I want to love without fear." So wrote one young woman, voicing a desire surely felt by the vast majority of people on the planet. Isn't this, in a sense, what being human is all about? We want to love in peace and security, not feeling that we have to hold back in case the other shoe drops. We want to make promises and receive promises, and be able to trust that both we and others will keep those promises. We want to open our hearts to love and know that we ourselves are loved in return.

Christian marriage is meant to be a place in which love can flourish without fear. It is intended to create families into which children can be welcomed, to provide a secure and life-giving context for sexual relationship, and to set in place a nurturing and supportive relationship between husband and wife. It is meant to be a setting in which human beings grow together into a love that is shaped by God's own love for his people.

But we live in a fallen world, and this does not happen automatically. The best of marriages are marked by shortcomings and imperfections. And when marriages go bad, they can go very bad indeed. The children of such marriages tend to be very deeply marked by the sorrow and suffering they have endured. They want so desperately to do better themselves and are often deeply skeptical as to whether better things are really possible.

In circumstances like these, how can we find the courage to love? One way to begin might be to remember the continuities between marriage and Christian life in general. Sometimes, what a marriage or any relationship needs is not an injection of big doses of excitement or inspiration. What it needs instead is more of the basic things that form the substance of the Christian life. Paul describes some of those things as the "fruit of the Spirit": love, joy, peace, patience, kindness, goodness, faithfulness, gentleness, self-control (Galatians 5:22-23).

One woman described for us an experiment she made in this regard. She had been married for fifteen years or so, and her life was full of all the normal challenges involved in keeping up with the various dimensions of her life: school, job, kids, aging parents, money worries—not to mention, of course, her husband and their marriage. She and a friend decided that for a week they would each try deliberately to say kind things to their husbands at every possible opportunity: "Thank you." "I appreciate that." "You did that so nicely." "I'm so sorry." "Let me help you." "Could you help me?"

At the end of the week, she and her friend met to compare notes. The effect on their family lives had been significant. It was as if the sun had come out. The stresses and strains were still there, but it was as if they and their spouses were working together on a beautiful day, rather than each laboring alone in the rain.

It is things like this that can help put the "Christian" back in marriage. Christians are not called to be heroic in marriage. We are called to be faithful and loving and imbued with the Spirit of Christ. When husbands and wives work together to cultivate the fruit of the Spirit, part of the harvest can be increased confidence that, yes, we can do it. It is all too easy for humans to fail to love each other well, but we can succeed in building marriages and families that reflect and participate in the redeeming love of God in Christ.

3

Families

Telling the Stories That Have Shaped Us

EVERY MARRIAGE FORMS A NEW FAMILY. That family does not appear out of nowhere. It is created by the union of two people who have each already been shaped by the families they grew up in. Getting married is thus more like the beginning of a new chapter than it is the beginning of a whole new book. None of us enters the story at the very beginning. As husbands and wives, we step into narratives that are already well underway and become coauthors of the next installment in the stories of each of our families.

For some people, the idea of continuing as adults a story begun by their parents and grandparents is a pleasant daydream. Their families are happy and stable, their parents were reliably nurturing, they were brought up in an atmosphere of love and support and encouragement. They would like nothing better than to grow up to be just like their parents.

For others, the thought that their future might be connected in any way with their family's past is more like a nightmare. Their parents' marriages are loveless, riven with conflict or simply non-existent. As much as these people might like to look to their families for support and guidance in matters of relationships or marriage, they feel that they cannot or must not do so. For them, the past is something to leave behind, not something to bring into the future.

For most of us, the reality of our families is somewhere between these two extremes. Most families possess both strengths and weaknesses, and their histories are marked by both joy and sorrow. And part of growing into adulthood is realizing that it is never possible simply to replicate the family formed by one's parents, no matter how exemplary it may have been, any more than it is possible simply to leave one's family history behind, no matter how problematic it may be.

Storytelling is a key element in moving into the future, whatever the nature of our pasts may be. We are creatures formed by stories—stories of our particular families, and the larger stories of creation and redemption. Those larger narratives are themselves family stories: on the one hand of the human family, and on the other of God's own family. If we are to be able to make sense of who we are and where we are going, we need to think about these stories. Whatever timeless principles we may believe we can extract from our family histories, those principles are no substitute for the stories themselves.

Scripture itself teaches us this by example. When God gives the law to the children of Israel, he tells them at the same time that one day their children will ask what that law means. When that happens, the people of Israel are to reply not with definitions or theories but with a story: "We were Pharaoh's slaves in Egypt; and the LORD brought us out of Egypt with a mighty hand" (Deuteronomy 6:21). The words accompanying the central act of Christian worship are a story: "The Lord Jesus on the night when he was betrayed took bread, and when he had given thanks, he broke it" (1 Corinthians 11:23-24).

Storytelling has been a necessary element in helping God's people live faithfully as members of his family since biblical times. It is just as necessary as an ingredient in helping us live in the present as faithful members of our own families. What then are the stories that we have to tell? What are the stories of our own families? What are some of the stories of the family of God as it has existed from its beginnings until now? And what shape might all of these stories take as they move from the past and into a future that is shaped by God's redemptive work in Christ?

Family Storytelling

We all learn our first lessons about being a member of a family from the families we grow up in. Those families and their ways of being in the world become our benchmarks for what counts as normal family life. The definition of normal differs, of course, from family to family. Families may be large or small, boisterous or quiet, oriented toward business or teaching or construction or farming. And families are shaped by their particular histories. Things happen in families, and nothing is ever the same again. Family storytelling allows people to identify and describe the events and patterns that have formed their families and thus their own perceptions of what family life is like.

The purpose of family storytelling is not to label the family as either "good" or "bad." The purpose is to tell the truth, in as nuanced and thoughtful a way as possible. This can be a complex undertaking, particularly for individuals who are just becoming adults. During young adulthood, many of us become newly privy to information about our families—information that may have been withheld from us when we were children, but that our parents or other relatives have now begun to share with us. How are we to make sense of it all?

Family storytelling can be scary as well as complex. We live in a fallen world, and there are no families in which there are no shadows. In some families there are more shadows than light. Those shadows do not necessarily mean that anyone is doing anything wrong. They can mean simply that people have suffered, and are suffering. That is hard enough to look at and to be honest about. But sometimes the shadows are linked to identifiable wrongdoing and interpersonal harm that has been perpetrated within the family circle. Telling—and hearing—the truth about such things can require a great deal of courage.

If your family is a happy one, it can seem disloyal to identify or discuss anything negative. If your family is sad, talking about the sadness may seem overwhelming. If your family does not talk about the past, it may be nerve-racking to look into it—who knows what you might find? Or perhaps you know very well what you will find. But it is worth doing. We bring ourselves and all of our stories into all our relationships, and so do those with whom we are in relationship. A willingness to tell our own stories, and to listen with compassion and patience and good humor to the stories of others, can be a key element in learning to live in intimate relationship, whether with friends or with a spouse.

Among Christians, there can be a tendency to expect all reasonably happy, functional families to be more or less alike. A "Christian family," it is assumed, will look and act a certain way. But even families that are superficially quite similar can have vastly different stories. And if your family are Italian Catholics from New Jersey, and your friend's family are Mennonites from central Pennsylvania, you are going to have a lot of talking and listening to do before you can even comfortably be guests in one another's homes, and much more if you want to consider marrying each other.

It can also be tempting to assume that certain kinds of difficulties do not occur in Christian families. Sometimes such assumptions are made by people whose families are in fact unaffected by these difficulties. At least as often, however, such beliefs are held by those whose families do in fact display these problematic characteristics. The shared consequence is dissonance between what individuals believe a Christian family is like, and what some families are in fact like.

A result of that dissonance is often a profound sense of loneliness and isolation for the members of families affected by difficult circumstances. Everyone else's family is perfect, they think, and mine is the only troubled one. Their reluctance to speak truthfully about their difficult circumstances is met by an equal reluctance on the part of others to hear the truth spoken. The assumption too easily made by everyone is that the Christian life is happy and victorious, and if yours isn't, you should at least have the decency to cover it up.

This is surely not what Jesus had in mind when he said, "You will know the truth, and the truth will make you free" (John 8:32). A reluctance to speak truthfully of sad things, or to hear those things spoken of, too often results in continued enslavement to the things Jesus came to free people from: sin, sorrow, fear, the kinds of brokenness that can be handed down in families for generations because no one can bear either to reach out for or to offer the kind of help that might lead to better things.

What kinds of problems are we talking about? One thread that we find woven through many family stories is that of father absence. Christian family ideals hold fathers in high regard, but many children grow up in homes in which fathers are either actually or functionally absent. It is common to think of father absence as being a product of divorce, and of course there are many families in which parents have divorced, children have remained with their mothers, and fathers have either disappeared or been marginalized in their children's experience.

But fathers are absent for other reasons as well. A lot of fathers who have stayed married to their children's mothers are nonetheless absent from those children's lives because they are at work. The Christian exaltation of the stay-at-home mother has a flip side that is not so often talked about: the always-at-work dad. The children of such parents often express powerful feelings of ambivalence toward their fathers, who they know worked long hours or traveled many weeks out of the year specifically so their wives could stay home with the children, but who thereby denied the children their own presence. The sons of such fathers feel they never had anyone to show them how to be men. The daughters of such fathers feel they never had anyone to answer the longings of their hearts for a father's love.

Fathers also die. In some families all the men seem to die young, leaving children not only fatherless but without uncles or grandfathers. And when a father dies who was already absent because of divorce or absorption in work or for some other reason, the wound is even deeper than it might otherwise have been. How can you grieve for someone who was already lost to you, whom you never really knew? How do you mourn the loss of a relationship that was never really there? Is it possible to reconcile anger toward an absent father with grief for a dead father?

A second thread woven through many stories has to do with what we might call sexual irregularities. Christian sexual ideals begin with premarital virginity and end with marital fidelity, but the reality of human sexual behavior is a lot more complicated than that. Many families are disrupted by adultery. Fathers have affairs, mothers have affairs, grandmothers and grandfathers and aunts and uncles have affairs. "Is my family just weird?" one young woman asked. "I don't understand why so many people cheat on their spouses."

Many families have also been affected by premarital pregnancy.

Members of older generations may have married because a baby was on the way; members of the current generation may have done the same. In many cases these pregnancies have been viewed as scandalous and shameful, and sometimes whole webs of lies have been constructed in an attempt to conceal the relative dates of weddings and the births of firstborns.

These sexual issues surface in the rearing of children. In families where infidelity is commonplace, children learn to expect it. Sometimes they are explicitly taught to expect it. "My fiancé tells me that he would never cheat," wrote one woman, "but my grandmother tells me that all men do it." In other families, parents are anxious that children should do as they say and not as they did. This can get very confusing for the children, particularly when parents are not forthcoming about what they did. Daughters sometimes grow up mystified by their mothers' strictness about boys and what they are and are not allowed to do with boys. Only later does it come out that the mothers had in their youth transgressed the very limits they were attempting to impose on their daughters. In such cases the daughter is often less shocked than she is relieved to learn the truth—now at last she understands why her mother has been so exercised about this for all these years.

A third dark thread is that of violence. For many Christians, domestic violence and child abuse are among the great unmentionables. Things like that just don't happen in Christian homes. But for too many young people, things like that are precisely what happen in their homes. One young woman told of her experience:

> My father led the singing every Sunday at my church. Then on Monday, Tuesday, Wednesday, Thursday, Friday and Saturday, he led the beatings and verbal abuse that went on in my house. No one suspected anything, and even if they had, it's hard for me to believe that anything would have been

done about it. There was this silent rule that no one inter-
feres with the family problems of others.

The silence of the church concerning violence in the home
leads even its victims to be uncertain whether anything is really
wrong. We have lost count of the number of individuals who have
recounted to us stories of family violence, at the same time ques-
tioning whether family violence is really part of their experience.
"My earliest memories of my father are of him screaming at my
mother and breaking all the dishes and doors in our home," wrote
one woman. "I didn't think the book we read on domestic violence
would have much to do with my life. 'Domestic violence' isn't a
term my family uses. We just talk about 'bad temper.'"

Children who grow up in violent homes learn to be victims,
and they learn to be perpetrators. What they do not learn is how
to be in relationships in which power is shared and dignity is respected. Midway through the semester one young man confided to
us that one of his first memories was of his father throwing his
mother to the ground and breaking her collarbone. "During our
first class, you asked why we were here," he wrote. "I lied. I forget
what I said, but it was not the truth. I am here because I do not
know what a healthy family looks like. I do not know what it
means to be a husband or a father."

A final thread that we find woven through many family stories
is that of secrecy. Secrecy is different from privacy. A private matter is something properly spoken of only to persons who need or
ought to know, or whom you wish to take into your confidence. A
secret, on the other hand, is something that must not be voiced to
anyone. Families make secrets of things that might otherwise be
simply private when they find the truth too painful or too embarrassing to bear.

Sometimes everyone knows what the secrets are and is well

aware that certain subjects are unmentionable. In other cases family members don't even realize they have secrets, even as they are busy keeping them. One woman confessed to being shocked by some of the stories of hurting families that her fellow students shared in class. "I thought, 'It's nice being in a family without any secrets.' And then it hit me, right in the middle of class. Our family has a huge secret that is never talked about. It is like a big fat elephant, and it attends every family gathering even though it was never invited."

Many family secrets have to do with matters of sex or violence. The lesbian sister, the gay uncle, the baby given for adoption, the half-sibling born of an affair, the father jailed for assault, the grandmother battered for decades before finally divorcing an abusive husband—these are things that many families find very difficult to talk about. So they don't. The hope, apparently, is that if you don't acknowledge it, it isn't there.

Children pick up on this. They learn to wonder whether the things their families never speak of are really there. Can they trust their senses and their memories? Or should they believe, as the rest of the family appears to believe, that the family has no secrets and no problems? Children also learn not to ask questions. The family is already tense; asking questions will only raise the tension level. And they might learn of something that they are better off not knowing. So they don't ask.

Sometimes, however, children do ask questions. And sometimes parents or other relatives tell the truth. The results can be transformative. "The day I found out is the day everything began to make sense," one person wrote. "My family is one of the least drama-filled I've ever known," wrote another. "If we have a secret like this, I can only imagine what else is out there. I have realized what really matters in a family." What really matters is that family members, by telling and hearing their family stories with honesty and courage, can love one another in the light of truth, not in the shadows of secrecy.

The "Biblical Family"

Certain sectors of the Christian church tend to construct a particular vision of the family and its place in the world, calling this idealized vision "the biblical family." This biblical family generally includes a husband and a wife, two-point-five children and a dog. The father goes out to work; the mother stays home. Perhaps the children go to a Christian school; perhaps they are homeschooled. If they go to public school, the family worries about the negative influences they may be encountering there. The family lives in the suburbs in a house with a two-car garage. They attend a church with a big parking lot and a youth group that meets on Wednesday nights. They are skittish about Halloween and skeptical of Santa Claus, but they love Memorial Day, Veterans Day and the Fourth of July. And they believe that biblical families like their own are the bedrock upon which both strong churches and a strong nation must be built.

Of course this is a caricature, but it is not much of one. In particular, the urge to idealize the nuclear family and to see the well-being of that kind of family as intimately related to the success of both church and state is characteristic of large sectors of the contemporary church. How appropriate are this idealization and this vision? What kinds of families do we really encounter in the Bible? And what kind of relationship between the family, the church and the broader society do we find portrayed in Scripture?

We find in Christian Scripture that its most prominent families bear no resemblance to the modern American nuclear family. Biblical families were large, and they lived not in individual units consisting of mother, father and young children, but in households that included adult children, in-laws, grandchildren, ser-

vants and livestock. Abraham had three wives and eight sons
(Genesis 16:3-4; 25:1-2). Isaac had "a great household, so that the
Philistines envied him" (Genesis 26:14). His son Esau had five or
six wives, at least five sons and an unspecified number of daughters (Genesis 26:34; 28:9; 36:1-6). Esau's twin, Jacob, had two
wives and two concubines, twelve sons, at least one daughter, and
a household that by the time of their journey into Egypt num-
bered seventy persons, not counting all the daughters-in-law
(Genesis 46:26-27).

Biblical families were also not "successful," if by success we
mean that they managed to avoid the kind of behavior that is commonly thought today to bring scandal upon the family or the
church. Abraham took a concubine when it appeared that God
was not coming through with the promised son fast enough (Genesis 16:1-3). His son Isaac learned from his father to tell lies about
his wife (Genesis 20:1-2; 26:6-7). Isaac's son Jacob colluded with
his mother to deceive both his brother and his father (Genesis 27).
Jacob's firstborn son, Reuben, had sexual relations with one of his
father's concubines (Genesis 35:22). Another of Jacob's sons, Joseph, was so overtly favored by his father that his brothers sold
him into slavery and then faked his death (Genesis 37).

Things don't really improve after the age of the patriarchs. The
judge Jephthah, apparently forgetting that Israelites were not supposed to sacrifice people, vowed that if he were victorious in battle
he would sacrifice whoever came out of his house first to greet
him upon his return. When that person turned out to be his
daughter, he followed through and sacrificed her (Deuteronomy
18:9-10; Judges 11:29-40). King David committed adultery and fa-
thered a child with another man's wife, and then arranged for her
husband to be killed in battle (2 Samuel 11:1-17). King Solomon,
that master of excess, had seven hundred wives and three hundred concubines (1 Kings 11:3). His son Rehoboam, with only

eighteen wives and sixty concubines, seems positively restrained by comparison (2 Chronicles 11:21). And then there is the heartbreaking story of Hosea and his adulterous wife, Gomer, whose marriage becomes a parable of God's sorrow over the unfaithfulness of his people, Israel (Hosea 1–2).

In the New Testament we do not find the enormous polygamous families that characterize at least the earlier portions of the Old Testament. But neither do we find much apparent interest in airbrushing the blemishes from the family portrait. The opening passage of the Gospel of Matthew is a genealogy that traces the descent of Jesus through the male line but includes four women along the way, each of whose stories sheds potentially embarrassing light on the family: Tamar (who was treated unjustly by her father-in-law and then impregnated by him when he took her for a prostitute), Rahab (who really was a prostitute), Ruth (a foreigner) and Bathsheba (whom Matthew refers to as "the wife of Uriah," as if he wants to make sure the reader remembers just exactly how inappropriate David's relations with her were) (Matthew 1:1-17).

We also do not find in the New Testament much in the way of a detailed blueprint for Christian families to follow. It seems to be assumed that people marry, and that husbands and wives may need encouragement to give themselves sexually to one another (1 Corinthians 7:1-6). No one is obliged to marry, and singleness may be preferable for some (1 Corinthians 7:25-31). Widows may remain single or may remarry (1 Corinthians 7:39-40; 1 Timothy 5:3-16). Christians do best to marry fellow Christians (2 Corinthians 6:14), but a Christian with an unbelieving spouse need not divorce simply for that reason (1 Corinthians 7:12-16). Husbands and wives are to submit to one another, recognizing that marriage is a parable of the relationship between Christ and the church (Ephesians 5:21-32). Household members (which are assumed to include servants or slaves as well as spouses and children) are to treat one another in ways consonant with the gospel (Colossians 3:18–4:1; 1 Peter 2:18–3:7).

What we do find in the New Testament are frequent suggestions that the family that takes precedence in the story of redemption is God's own family, which is formed not by marriage or by blood relationship but by faith and adoption (Mark 3:32-35; Romans 8:19-23; Galatians 4:3-7). In Scripture that family is called "the household of faith" or "the household of God" or simply "the church" (Galatians 6:10; 1 Timothy 3:15). Membership in this family does not erase the natural loyalties that human beings feel toward people to whom they are related by kinship or by marriage, but it profoundly relativizes those loyalties. So significant a point is this that Jesus regularly resorts to hyperbole when making it: "Call no man your father on earth, for you have one Father, who is in heaven" (Matthew 23:9); "Leave the dead to bury their own dead; but as for you, go and proclaim the kingdom of God" (Luke 9:60). "If any one comes to me and does not hate his own father and mother and wife and children and brothers and sisters, yes, and even his own life, he cannot be my disciple" (Luke 14:26).

To a people whose God-given law had long stressed the importance of honoring parents and spouses, this must have seemed extremely strange. Wasn't marriage a solemn religious duty? Weren't children's responsibilities toward parents equally solemn religious duties? Yes, of course. But as Jesus points out, human families are good but not ultimate. In the age to come, people will neither marry nor be given in marriage (Luke 20:34-35). There will not be lots of brides and grooms in the kingdom of heaven: there will be one bridegroom, Jesus, and one bride, the church (Matthew 25:1-13; Revelation 21:2).[1]

Human marriages and families are thus not ends in them-

---

[1]See also Matthew 9:15; 22:1-14; Mark 2:19; Luke 5:34; John 3:29; 2 Corinthians 11:2.

selves; rather, they are forms under which human beings can be members of the family of God, moving together toward the day when they all, as Christ's bride, will be united with their bridegroom. This relativizing of marital and parental bonds suggests that there is no one superior way to be a Christian. Marriage and parenthood are fine things, but the unmarried and the childless are equally called to be disciples of Jesus and equally members of the household of God.

It is not clear that the contemporary church really believes this, given the number of churches that trumpet their orientation toward "ministering to families." But the modern Western nuclear family consisting of a husband, a wife and their children is simply too narrow and culture-specific a family form to merit identification as "the biblical family." It is culture-specific, in that such families exist only in societies with industrial economies that make it possible for nuclear family units (or single persons, for that matter) to survive in isolation from larger webs of extended family or other sorts of community. This is why there are no nuclear families in the Bible—the economic and technological conditions of the ancient world did not permit it. Indeed, there are plenty of places in the world today where people do not live in nuclear families, because their social and economic contexts dictate that families take other forms.

The modern Western nuclear family is, likewise, too narrow a conception of family to be identified as uniquely "biblical" because Scripture strongly indicates that God includes everyone in his family, whatever form his or her earthly family may take. Jesus did not go around calling only married parents to be his disciples, or suggesting that the success of the kingdom of God depended on them. On the contrary, Jesus told people that whatever their family loyalties were, they had to set them aside if they wanted to be his disciples. This sweeping rejection of the prior claims of spouse or parents or children opens the door to people in any and every family situation being freed for the service of God and for membership in his family.

To put it another way: the biblical family is not a married couple and their children. The biblical family is the church. And the mission of the church is not to provide services to human families. Even less is the church's mission to support the broader society—what we might call the state or the nation—by serving the family. The mission of the church is to make disciples who can bear faithful witness to the redeeming and transforming work of God in Christ. To the extent that ministries to children or to couples can help make such disciples, so much the better. But marriages and families cannot be the focus of the life of the church. Marriages and families find their meaning as the vision of their members is lifted beyond the horizon of their own households to that of the household of God and, beyond that, to the kingdom of God itself.

Christian Families

So what does a Christian family look like? How can you tell when the Christian character of a family goes deeper than the Bible verses they might have displayed on their walls? One approach might be to ask in what ways a particular family reflects the kinds of qualities that are supposed to characterize God's own family. Of course no human family will ever possess any such quality in all of its fullness and perfection. But thinking about families in this way can help us to consider how the families in which we grew up approximated the shape of the Christian life, and how they may have fallen short. It can also help us to think about what aspects of our family legacy we wish to retain in our own adult lives, what aspects we want to leave behind, and what new things we might feel drawn toward.

Prominent among qualities that ought to characterize a Christian family is hospitality.[2] God welcomes us when we are yet strangers; he makes us members of his family and gives us a place at his table. Thus as Christians we are invited to practice hospitality, welcoming the alien and the stranger, and as we do so remembering Christ's own words: "As you did it to one of the least of these my brethren, you did it to me" (Matthew 25:40).

Even apart from any consideration of children or the broader community, hospitality is an essential virtue in Christian marriage. There is no one so strange as the person you marry. It is easy to love in our partners those characteristics that we find attractive and easy to understand. But the more intimately we know one another, the more inevitable it becomes that we will learn things about each other that we find not so attractive and not so easy to understand. Can we continue to offer each other a place at the table, even as we begin to realize how complex and at least partially incomprehensible the other is?

When hospitality is lacking, family members can feel like outsiders. The source of the alienation might be a function of personality—for example, a quirky sense of humor that no one else in the family quite seems to get. It might be a function of birth order, of having felt lost in the shuffle as the middle child or the youngest child. It might be something that seems to run contrary to the self-understanding of the family—a rejection of the Christian faith shared by the rest of the family, or a lifestyle that is openly or not-so-openly gay.

Too often the response of families to the black sheep among them is a mixture of cluelessness (they have no idea why these individuals feel this way), resentment (it is so awkward to have family members who don't fit in) and a shifting of responsibility

---

[2]For this delineation of the characteristics of a Christian family, we are indebted to Herbert Anderson and Susan B. W. Johnson, *Regarding Children* (Louisville: Westminster John Knox, 1994), pp. 72-90.

(if these others would only change, then things would be better).
But it may be that if anything is going to change for the better,
these outsiders need to be shown hospitality now, just as they are.
Jesus ate with tax collectors and sinners, and Scripture does not
record that he did so with his teeth gritted. Can we as Christians
make room at our family tables even for our black sheep?

A second quality that ought to mark a Christian family is compassion. God in Christ bore the burden of human sin, suffering
with us and for us, and in so doing redeeming us from the power
of sin and death. As Christians we are called to imitate Christ's
sufferings, bearing one another's burdens and thus participating
in the mystery of redemption.

One of the first opportunities that Christian spouses or future
spouses have to learn compassion in relationship with one another is in speaking of past losses and mourning those losses with
one another. Everyone has suffered, and everyone brings suffering
with him or her into relationship. But talking about happiness is a
lot easier than talking about sorrow. It takes courage to be willing
both to speak and to hear sad things, and to extend and receive
compassion for wounds that may be largely healed or that may
still be fresh and painful.

Compassion does not happen automatically. One common barrier to compassion is posed by the temptation to keep our sorrows
to ourselves, and the corresponding temptation to avert our eyes
from the sufferings of others or to offer solutions rather than sympathy. Our society is both highly individualistic and highly technological; we expect people to solve their own problems and all
problems to be solvable. When situations arise in which there is
no quick fix, it can seem less embarrassing to everyone if the
problems are just kept under wraps. Husbands and wives hide
their sorrows from each other; married couples hide their sorrows
from friends and extended family. And when suffering is a secret,

compassion is rendered difficult, if not impossible. You cannot help to bear a burden you know nothing about.

Another barrier to compassion is disapproval. It is hard to be compassionate toward people whose behavior you find unacceptable; it is easier to hope they get what they deserve. But it is possible for individuals and families to find the strength and grace to respond compassionately to a family member in some sort of nonrespectable crisis: trouble with the law, or with alcohol or drugs or sex or money. In many cases families look back to those compassionate responses as turning points in their shared history, as times when things began slowly but decisively to change for the better. God's mercy comes to all of us as people who need it. As Christians we too are called to extend compassion not just to the deserving but to everyone.

A third quality that ought to characterize a Christian family is justice. God's dealings with people are always characterized by justice. God is truthful and straightforward in communicating his standards and desires to his people. He is not capricious; his rules do not change from one day to the next or from one set of people to the next. God is grieved by injustice wherever it occurs, desiring that people should treat one another justly both within the household of faith and beyond its borders. Christians ought to strive to mirror the justice of God in their individual lives and in the common lives of their families.

In a just family, people know what the rules are, and the rules apply to everyone. Fairness, honesty, kindness and respect characterize the dealings of family members with one another, with no one seen as deserving less of these than any other. Justice also goes beyond rules. A Christian family should be a place where children are taught by example to recognize how complex people and situations are, and to form habits of nuanced moral reflection and action.

In a just family, conflict is dealt with openly and constructively.

People find ways to be angry without being mean; they find ways to listen to one another without requiring that whoever is upset must scream and yell to get the others' attention. They find ways to resolve conflict that involve not just the exercise of power by whoever has more of it, but instead a coming together of persons in cooperative problem-solving efforts.

Double standards are incompatible with justice. When one spouse demands respect but does not give it, when parents require that children do as they say but not as they do, when rules are in force at some times but not at others, the message is clear: don't expect fairness in this family. Secrecy is profoundly injurious to justice as well. If there are family rules against telling the truth, everyone lives in a fog of uncertainty in which it is impossible for victims of injustice to seek protection or redress.

Truth telling can be an essential first step in pursuing justice within and as a family. What is really going on? Does everyone tell the story the same way, or are there widely differing perceptions of what the family is about? Simply papering over those differences may seem comfortable, but it is unlikely to conduce to real fairness or unity within the family circle. Justice requires first being truthful about possible reasons for discord.

And finally, reconciliation should be a practice of any Christian family. Reconciliation lies at the heart of the gospel itself. Sin separates humans from God and from each other. The history of redemption is all about God tearing down the walls that have come to exist between humans and himself and rebuilding the bonds that ought to bind God and humans to one another in peaceable community.

When people get married, peaceable community tends to be near the top of the list of things they are hoping for, although they may call it by some other name: "getting along," for example. But getting along is not always easy, even with someone you love. Even well-intentioned people can fail each other or hurt each other, in small ways and in large. If marriages and families are to thrive, spouses and family members have to find redemptive ways of dealing with these hurts and failures.

Reconciliation usually requires a deliberate effort to deal with problems or perceived problems. Sometimes it can seem more pious simply to let things go; part of wisdom does lie in discerning when small things really are small and ought to be let go. But particularly when spouses are young or have not yet established habits of dealing constructively with conflict and misunderstandings and hurt feelings, letting things go can be very dangerous. It can easily produce not peace itself but the illusion of peace, and underneath that illusion very destructive storms can be brewing.

There are things that can make reconciliation harder. Grudges, for instance, are a common barrier to reconciliation. Sometimes people do not want to let go of the harm that has been done to them, or that they perceive has been done to them. Sometimes they do not want to let go of their status as victims, feeling that this is more satisfying than whatever the alternatives might be. Sometimes people do not want to rebuild trust after a betrayal, even when the offending party is truly sorry and truly desires to move forward into better things.

Sometimes, though, the offending party is not truly sorry. He or she may not be sorry at all, or may feign sorrow only as a means toward being granted forgiveness, after which he or she expects things to go on as usual. This is another common and powerful barrier to reconciliation. Christians are commanded by God to forgive. But we are also commanded to repent of our sins, not to make excuses for them, and not to underestimate the damage that they do. When those who inflict wounds make light of them, healing is unlikely to occur.

Reconciliation is not always possible. Sometimes repentance is lacking. Sometimes forgiveness is lacking, and sometimes so much damage has been done to the relationship or to one or more of the individuals involved that no amount of forgiveness and repentance can open the way to reconciliation in this life.

These limits to the scope and possibility of reconciliation are matched by similar limits in other dimensions of Christian family life. No family is ever going to be perfectly just, or perfectly compassionate, or perfectly hospitable. Not in this life. People have limits; families have limits; marriages have limits. This is part of what it means to be a creature, and not God himself. If our motivation in seeking to build Christian marriages and families is a desire for perfection here and now, we are going to be perpetually disappointed.

But if our motivation is a desire to model our family lives on the life of God's family, and to open ourselves and our marriages and families to the workings of God's grace, we may find that even with all our limitations and imperfections, powerfully good things can be possible. Hospitality, compassion, justice and reconciliation can become realities in our lives and in our families, and we may find ourselves astonished at the transforming possibilities they bring with them.

Memory and Hope

Most of us receive a mixed legacy from the families in which we grew up. There are good things and there are bad things. In a best-case scenario, the good far outweighs the bad. Where this is the case, people feel a sense of empowerment and possibility as they embark upon adulthood and adult decisions about when and how to form new families of their own. They are not afraid to remember their family's story, and they are full of hope for the future.

In other cases the scenario is not so rosy. Sometimes families have been marked by serious failure and suffering, often in patterns that have been in place for generations. People who grow up in such families often feel that their own adulthood is doomed before it even begins. They feel that whatever negative things have happened in their families are bound to happen to them. They are pained by their family's past, and hardly dare to hope for their own future.

For all of us, memory and hope go hand in hand. We need to remember the good, and we need to remember the bad, in whatever proportions they were and are present in our families. Even when much of the story is positive, we need the revealing light of the gospel to help us be truthful about the dark threads that are also a part of it, and to help us put our confidence not in the human goodness of our family but in the transforming power of God's grace.

And when much of the story is negative, that same revealing light of the gospel can show us not only the darkness that we have lived through but also the hope that is possible even for our own lives. Simply beginning to tell honestly the story of one's family can prove a powerful first step in choosing something better for oneself. An untold story is "just the way it is." Only once the story has been given words can a person begin to imagine that story continuing in different ways.

Christian Scripture speaks of marriage as a process of "leaving" and "cleaving": "Therefore a man leaves his father and his mother and cleaves to his wife" (Genesis 2:24). Learning to tell the stories of our families can be an important element in both of these processes. It is far easier to step into adulthood and adult relationships when you have a sense of your family legacy and how it has shaped you. And it is far easier to form a new family when you and your spouse are aware of what each of you brings to that new family. A great deal of the challenge and delight of marriage comes in navigating those legacies and building a marriage whose uniqueness lies partly in how the stories of your two families have been knit together.

4

Peace

Handling Conflict Constructively

No two people are the same. In that simple, obvious truth lie the roots of some of the greatest pleasures of life, and at the same time some of life's greatest challenges. People have different strengths and different interests, different ideas and different abilities. One of the reasons individuals are drawn to marriage is that we expect to enjoy and benefit from the ways in which our spouses are different from ourselves. We expect marriage to have a richness and variety that would be harder to find in a single life.

But individuals and their particularities do not always mesh neatly. In the imperfect world we inhabit, differences inevitably give rise to conflict. Different strengths lead to competition rather than cooperation. Different needs lead to resentment rather than to willing mutual service. And the anticipated richness of life together can descend into something that looks more like chaos than like concord.

Peace, it turns out, does not just happen. Differences do not resolve themselves automatically. If husbands and wives are to live in harmony with one another, they cannot just sit back and hope for the best—they must actively cultivate peace. Conflicts must be acknowledged and then negotiated in ways that are constructive rather than destructive, and that allow the relationship to grow and change and become stronger and better than it was before.

This is not a lesson that all of us learn at home. In some families, it seems that people irritate each other on purpose. "I hate going home," one young woman confessed. "My parents are always having petty fights. I don't like it, but what can you say to your parents—'Children, behave'?" In other homes, fights may start small, but they end big. "As a young child, I can remember listening to my parents fight," wrote another woman. "It was as if they were continuously throwing more logs on the fire, instead of attempting to remove those that were already burning."

The obvious ugliness of such scenarios is undoubtedly why some people try to manage conflict by avoiding it altogether. Better just not to talk about things that might lead to an argument. If you don't know what the other person thinks, you can't fight about it. "I try as hard as I can to avoid conflicts," wrote one young man. "My thinking is that it is better if fights do not take place, and everyone is left in a state of ignorance, but of a peaceful sort."

The biggest problem with this strategy is that it doesn't work. Conflict avoidance is not conflict resolution, however much we might like it to be. "I find myself not wanting to disagree, thinking that will promote unity and togetherness," an engaged man wrote. "So even when I see a problem, I let it fester, assuming it will somehow work itself out and disappear with no harm done. I can't say I've ever seen that happen with any remotely serious matter, but somehow the belief remains."

But what if you try to deal with conflict, and then find yourselves unable to find your way out the other side? What if you talk and you talk and you talk, and you simply cannot agree? What if, the more you try to deal with your differences, the more differences you notice, until your marriage becomes, in the words of one woman, "one long, never-ending fight with little bits of temporary relief here and there"?

Faced with so unpleasant a prospect, it is no wonder that people find themselves casting about for a strategy to ensure that conflict can be resolved easily and reliably. A strategy adopted by some Christians is so-called traditional gender roles, a primary feature of which is the allocation of decision-making authority to the husband. As one young woman explains: "If a husband and wife are in conflict, the Bible advises that the husband should make the decision."

Does the Bible really teach this? And does this way of structuring the relationship of husband and wife really foster peaceable marriages? We don't think so. Construing scriptural teaching on marriage as having to do primarily—or even tangentially—with the allocation of power is fraught with interpretive and theological problems. And practically speaking, it just doesn't work. At best, assigning decision-making power to one partner in the marriage serves to short-circuit conflict, not to address it. At worst, it sets in place an ideology of control that can serve to underwrite and reinforce abuse and violence in intimate relationships.

There has to be a better way. "Blessed are the peacemakers," Jesus says, "for they shall be called [children] of God" (Matthew 5:9). What exactly is peace? What are ways in which Christian husbands and wives can seek to live at peace with one another, even as they navigate together whatever conflicts arise between them? How can they know when they are succeeding? What does it mean to be a peacemaker?

Violence in Relationships

In a perfect world, perhaps it would be possible to live in peace without having to think about violence. That is not the world in which we live. In our world, violence and abuse are at least as common and at least as visible as peace and peacefulness. And the line between peace and violence is not drawn between the church and the world, or between Christians and non-Christians. Abuse and violence, and the impulses that lead to them, are found even in Christian institutions and Christian relationships.

Officially, Christians have mostly deplored and sought to limit violence. In the early centuries of the church, most Christians were pacifists, believing that no follower of Jesus should wield the sword for any reason. After the conversion of the Emperor Constantine, many Christians became persuaded that serving in the army or on the police force of a Christian state was acceptable for a Christian. However, certain limitations (collectively known as "just-war theory") were understood to apply even to state-sponsored violence. Private vengeance was viewed as unacceptable, and weapons were barred from churches and monasteries, both of which symbolized the kingdom of God—a realm in which, it was anticipated, all swords would be beaten into plowshares and war would be made no more.

In our own day, limitations on violence have come to be seen by many—including many Christians—as a luxury that they cannot afford. If a state feels its security is threatened, it should be able to wage war by any means it deems necessary. If an individual feels his or her security is threatened, that person should be able to carry a gun. If a church feels its security is threatened, it should be able to arm its congregants.[1] This conviction that violence may sometimes simply be necessary is often expressed in hypothetical worst-case scenarios: suppose burglars break into your home and threaten to injure or kill your family members. If you had a weapon at hand, would you not be justified in shooting

---

[1]Electa Draper, "Weapons at Church? For Everything, There Is a Time," *Denver Post,* December 12, 2007.

these criminals? Might it even be your duty to do so?

This line of reasoning makes violence seem obviously necessary, at least in extreme circumstances. But if violence is appropriate in extreme circumstances, why not in less extreme circumstances? If violence is appropriate as a last resort, why not as a next-to-last resort, or even as a first resort? After all, who has the patience to wait until all other options have been exhausted? Why not just use however much force you have to use to get what you want, when you want it?

Media entertainment certainly portrays violence this way. In many television shows and movies, violence is not an element in a larger story; it is itself the story. These shows portray violence as spectacularly gory, but without any particular consequences, either legal or in terms of human suffering. And both perpetrators and victims are represented without moral nuance: there are only bad guys, who deserve whatever they get, and good guys, who are justified in whatever they dish out.[2] The message is clear: violence is not an exception to the rule; violence is the rule.

There are Christians who are deeply disturbed by the prevalence of violent imagery in popular culture. There are others who are enthusiastic consumers of it. One video game, violent enough that its sales are restricted to persons over seventeen, has come to be used by churches all across the country as a recruiting tool for youth groups. Is it really a good idea to give twelve-year-olds access—at church, no less—to a game that involves blowing people up? Well, as the pastor of one such church pointed out, no one is really getting shot. It is all just "pixels on a screen."[3]

Not all pixels are created equal, though. This argument is sel-

[2]Barbara Osborn, "Violence Formula: Analyzing TV, Video and Movies," *Media and Values* 62 (Spring 1993) <www.medialit.org/reading_room/article94.html>.
[3]Matt Richtel, "Thou Shalt Not Kill, Except in a Popular Video Game at Church," *New York Times*, October 7, 2007.

dom offered to excuse the consumption of, say, Internet pornography, or to defend its use as a youth-group recruitment tool. Most
people will say—publicly, at least—that they think imaginary,
computerized sex is bad for you. Why don't they think imaginary,
computerized violence is bad for you? Maybe because, at base, they
think sex is bad and violence is normal and unremarkable.

What might happen if we were to assume that violence is not
normal and should be noticed and resisted? How might our lives
be different if we were to think, not in terms of improbable worst-
case scenarios that might justify the use of violence or coercion,
but in terms of ordinary situations that we encounter all the time
and that we can, if we choose, meet with peace or with approaches
that might lead to peace?

One thing we might notice is how problematic a lot of our own
behavior and relationships are. We assume that in relationships a
certain level of meanness is to be expected. We make unkind remarks because we happen to feel like it. We lose our tempers and
find ways to excuse our angry outbursts or to blame them on the
other person. We attempt to manipulate and control situations or
people for the sake of getting what we want. When we don't get
what we want, we yell, or we sulk, or we issue threats or ultima-
tums and expect our partners to fall into line.

We accept behavior like this from one another, too. We make
excuses when people hurt us. The more we love the person, or believe that he or she loves us, the more excuses we make. We assume
that we must somehow be guilty, that the pain we are experiencing
must be our own fault. We believe we must be making a big deal
over something that really doesn't matter. After all, being in a relationship is a wonderful thing, right? We shouldn't get all nitpicky
about how we're treated in the context of that relationship.

This paves the way for abuse in intimate relationships. Dating
relationships don't start with abuse—they start with romance, or

what seems like romance. "We were involved very quickly; we met and were officially dating the next day," wrote one young woman. "At the time, I thought it was all very exciting and must have meant true love." Then came the verbal attacks, the jealousy, the controlling: what she could do, where she could go, whom she could talk to. "Now I look back on the relationship, and I see how messed up we were."

She and her partner were not alone. Intimate-partner violence (meaning violence against a current or former spouse, girlfriend or boyfriend) affects millions of Americans every year. In an estimated 85 percent of cases, it is women who are victims, and men who are their abusers. When women are victims, they are far more likely to be physically injured or killed by their abusers than are male victims.[4] And this problem is increasingly concentrated among the young: the age group with the highest per-capita rate of relationship violence is adolescents and young adults aged 16-24.[5]

Many young people involved in abusive relationships have learned to play their parts at home. When there is violence or abuse in the home, children (especially girls) learn to keep their heads down and appease the perpetrator. Other children (especially boys) learn that the way to be a man is to dominate women and children. When these children become old enough to enter into relationships of their own, too often they reprise the roles they have been taught, with young men seeking—intentionally or by instinct—partners they can easily dominate, and young women

---

[4]One in three female homicide victims is killed by a current or former husband or boyfriend, compared with one in thirty-five male homicide victims killed by a current or former wife or girlfriend. Family Violence Prevention Fund, "Get the Facts: The Facts on Domestic, Dating and Sexual Violence" <www.endabuse.org/content/action_center/detail/754>.

[5]Family Violence Prevention Fund, "The Facts on Teenagers and Intimate Partner Violence" <www.endabuse.org/userfiles/file/Children_and_Families/Teenagers.pdf>. See also Elizabeth Olson, "A Rise in Efforts to Spot Abuse in Youth Dating," *New York Times,* January 3, 2009.

being drawn to controlling men who evoke in them comfortably familiar patterns of submission.

In other instances the victims of relationship violence may come from peaceable homes but are caught in the crossfire of a culture that tolerates and glorifies violence, and left undefended by a church that fails to acknowledge the reality and danger of abuse in intimate relationships. One young woman recounted to us the story of her first dating relationship. She was fourteen; he was sixteen. Her friends thought it was cool that her boyfriend was older, and so did she. But after the warm fuzzies came the putdowns, the controlling, the isolation, the physical abuse: pushing her, hitting her, throwing things at her.

She was afraid to tell her parents, so she told her youth pastor. "He told me I was overreacting, and that this could not be happening." Two months after this, the boyfriend raped her. "At this point I didn't know what to do. If the youth pastor didn't believe me before, he was surely not going to believe me now. I was afraid to tell my parents, and afraid to tell anyone else. I kept this horrible secret inside." Eventually she did find someone who was willing to listen, to believe her, and to enlist her parents and the authorities in protecting her from her boyfriend, whose abuse by this time had escalated from rape to attempts at homicide.

Why was this teenager's pastor unwilling either to believe her or to protect her—by, for example, referring her to domestic-violence professionals in the community? Apparently he did not believe that her story could possibly be true. Perhaps he knew the boyfriend and believed him incapable of abuse. Perhaps he believed that abuse could not happen in his youth group, in his church, among people he knew. Perhaps he simply found it more comfortable to suppose that this young woman was lying than to grapple with the ugly reality of abuse.

Whatever his reason, he has lots of company. The numbers of

Christian clergy—and in particular those ministering to young people—who deal forthrightly with matters of abuse and domestic violence are vanishingly small. "Not once in my twenty-three, almost twenty-four, years of life do I ever remember a pastor teaching about abuse and abusive relationships," wrote a newly married man. "My youth group didn't mention it, and my college pastors still haven't mentioned it. Why the big secret?" "It is no wonder that people think domestic violence is not an issue for Christian families," wrote another individual. "No one ever talks about it."

This is not good enough. A concern for the quality of relationships and the health of families is central to the self-image of the vast majority of Christian individuals and Christian churches. That concern needs to translate into a willingness to acknowledge and to engage with the real challenges faced by real people. That includes the risks and realities of abuse in intimate relationships.

To put it another way: as Christians, we need to learn to recognize and respond appropriately to violence and abuse. We do not protect ourselves against fire by assuming a fire will never happen. On the contrary: we install smoke alarms, we hold fire drills, and we call the fire department if we so much as see a wisp of smoke issuing from behind a baseboard. We do so because we know that where there is smoke, there is fire, and if we leave it to smolder, it will kill us or other people.

So also with intimate-partner violence. Quick involvement, jealousy, attempts at control, demeaning remarks, isolation from family and friends, threats of violence, any actual violence of any kind—these are the warning signs that foreshadow more serious abuse. They are no more likely to go away by themselves than a house fire is likely to put itself out. And in many cases it can be harder to flee an abusive relationship than it is to flee a burning house. A burning house does not pursue a fleeing victim, but perpetrators of relationship violence commonly pursue theirs.[6]

The destructive and potentially lethal character of intimate-partner violence means that the appropriate response to such violence on the part of the Christian community—friends, family, youth workers, ministers—is to provide protection to the victim and accountability to the perpetrator. This will require working together with social-service and law-enforcement professionals. It will also involve making it plain, in both public and private settings, that violence and abuse are not acceptable in Christian relationships. The church is to be a place of peace and of safety for everyone, including in the contexts of marriage, family and dating relationships.[7]

Men, Women and Conflict

Violence is not inevitable—but conflict is. People will have different ideas about what to do, how to do it, and whether it is a good idea to be doing it at all. Some conflicts can be so trivial as to seem laughable. Should the toothpaste tube be squeezed from the bottom or the middle? Can the same sponge be used to wash the dishes and to wipe the counters? Is it better to turn up the thermostat or to put on a sweater?

But as anyone knows who has ever had an argument with a roommate or spouse about which way the toilet paper should go onto the holder, the triviality of a conflict is no guarantee that anyone is going to find it funny. On the contrary: trivial matters can become the battlegrounds upon which we act out more sig-

---

[6] At least half of the women who leave their abusers are followed and harassed or further attacked by them. The majority of men who kill their spouses do so after the couple has separated or divorced. See Mark Reutter, "Battered women who kill in non-beating situation have self-defense right," News Bureau: University of Illinois at Urbana-Champaign, September 1, 2005 <www.news.illinois.edu/II/05/0901/0901.pdf>.

[7] Helpful web resources include the website of the Faith Trust Institute <www.faith trustinstitute.org> and the page "Advocacy for Victims of Abuse" on the website of the Evangelical Covenant Church <www.covchurch.org/avabuse>.

nificant conflicts that may lie beneath the surface and that we have so far failed to address.

It may sometimes be that deeper conflicts remain unaddressed simply because we have not yet realized they are there. Surface-level conflicts can become invitations and opportunities to dig a little deeper and to try to figure out what is going on. Sometimes, though, we are hesitant to identify or address deeper conflicts precisely because they are nontrivial. We are afraid that if we look at them, they will engulf and destroy the relationship.

For many Christian young people, the fear that relationships will be disrupted or ended by conflict is itself not trivial. These young people are heirs to the culture of divorce, in which it seems that discord between spouses must inevitably lead to marital shipwreck. Is it possible, they wonder, to structure a marriage in such a way that conflict can be contained and resolved before it has a chance to reach destructive proportions?

Considerations of what Christian Scripture does and does not say about the relationship of husband and wife in marriage often come into play at this point. A biblical passage that is particularly significant in this respect is Ephesians 5:21-33: "Be subject to one another out of reverence for Christ. Wives, be subject to your husbands, as to the Lord. For the husband is the head of the wife as Christ is the head of the church. . . . Let each one of you [husbands] love his wife as himself, and let the wife see that she respects her husband."

Among some Christians this passage is understood as assigning decision-making power in any male-female intimate relationship to the man. In the words of one individual: "At home and at church, I was taught that Ephesians 5 meant that if there was a disagreement about a decision that needed to be made, the man made it. The woman's voice could be heard and considered, but the man in the relationship should make the final decision."

Often this conviction is couched in terms of "leadership" or
"spiritual leadership" or "servant leadership," all of which, it is
supposed, are synonymous with what Ephesians 5 means in
using the word *head*. Husbands are to be leaders. Boyfriends and
fiancés are too. What does this mean? It means they make the
decisions. In the words of another individual: "I have heard
many of my female friends state that they expect their husbands
to be their spiritual leaders and to make the ultimate decision in
an argument."

The appeal of this arrangement is that it seems to promise relationships in which conflict is resolved instantaneously and automatically, since the husband (or boyfriend) as "head" (or "leader") makes
all decisions in contested matters. It is therefore impossible for any
conflict to become intractable. Headship is a trump card, and the
man holds it. As soon as a husband and wife (or boyfriend and girlfriend) suspect they might not be able to agree, the man plays his
trump card, makes the decision, and the conflict evaporates.

Perhaps this is attractive as a fantasy—although perhaps it is
not even that. Ephesians 5 is one of the few passages of Christian
Scripture that speak directly to the duties of spouses to one another. To interpret this passage as if it has to do primarily, if not
exclusively, with control and acquiescence carries with it the
strong implication that marriage itself is an arrangement that is
primarily, if not exclusively, concerned with control and acquiescence. How positive a picture of marriage is this, really?

Positive or not, this is the picture that many Christians are
busy painting. Young people attend youth group meetings, read
books, and listen to wedding homilies in which they are advised
that, in Christian relationships, men are to lead and women are to
follow. It is unseemly, they are told, for a Christian woman to take
any initiative or make any decisions. When women exercise control, men feel disrespected. A wife's duty is thus to cede control to

her husband. He will then feel respected, and she will feel loved.[8]

How does this actually work? In real life, not very well. Even when people articulate these ideals, they often do not live up to them. "My mother always used to teach male headship," wrote one individual. "She would say that my father was supposed to be the spiritual leader of the household, and the leader in every other way too. Truth be told, my mother is in charge of basically everything in my family." When they do live up to these ideals, marriages do not then automatically succeed. "My mother and my father had a relationship in which neither of them thought that it was ever appropriate for her to tell him 'no,'" wrote another person. Her parents had by then been divorced for years.

Things are just as frustrating at the dating stage. Men can't figure out what it is they are supposed to be doing as the "spiritual leaders" in their relationships, and feel burdened and isolated by the obligation they feel to be decision makers. Women can't figure out why they can't find men who are willing to be leaders, or why the men they do find don't want to make the decisions. One young woman explained,

> In my relationship with my first boyfriend, my expectation was that the man should be more of the decision maker. This is not saying I didn't want to be involved, but I thought that as a "Christian woman" I was supposed to let the man lead the relationship. It became a constant battle: "You need to

---

[8]For a selection of books that make these points, see Emerson Eggerich, *Love and Respect: The Love She Most Desires; The Respect He Desperately Needs* (Nashville: Thomas Nelson, 2004); John Eldredge, *Wild at Heart: Discovering the Secret of a Man's Soul* (Nashville: Thomas Nelson, 2001); John Eldredge and Stasi Eldredge, *Captivating: Unveiling the Mystery of a Woman's Soul* (Nashville: Thomas Nelson, 2005); Elisabeth Elliott, *Passion and Purity: Learning to Bring Your Love Life Under Christ's Control* (Grand Rapids: Revell, 1984); Shaunti Feldhahn, *For Women Only: What You Need to Know About the Inner Lives of Men* (Sisters, Ore.: Multnomah, 2004); Shaunti Feldhahn and Jeff Feldhahn, *For Men Only: A Straightforward Guide to the Inner Lives of Women* (Sisters, Ore.: Multnomah, 2006).

make the decision!" "I don't want to make the decision; you make the decision!" And at the end of the day, no decisions had been made.

In our judgment, the principal reason why this way of construing male-female relationships works so poorly in practice is because it is fatally flawed in theory. Marriage is not fundamentally about conflict and control. Headship and submission are not about decision making and acquiescence. And Ephesians 5 has nothing to do with "spiritual leadership" or "servant leadership" or any other kind of leadership, at least insofar as leadership is construed as decision-making authority.

The New Testament actually has very little to say about leadership-as-power, and what it does say is not positive. In Matthew 20, Jesus says,

> The rulers of the Gentiles lord it over them, and their great men exercise authority over them. It shall not be so among you; but whoever would be great among you must be your servant, and whoever would be first among you must be your slave; even as the Son of man came not to be served but to serve, and to give his life as a ransom for many. (Matthew 20:25-28)

This is not a recommendation of "servant leadership." It is a recommendation of servanthood, period.

Headship, too, is not promoted in the New Testament as a means by which one person imposes his or her will on another. In 1 Corinthians 11:3, the apostle Paul points to God the Father and Jesus Christ as the model for husbands and wives in this regard, and it is most emphatically not the case that God the Father is in the business of making decisions on behalf of the Holy Trinity when the Father and the Son are unable to reach agreement in any other way.

On the contrary: the relationship of the Father and the Son is characterized in Scripture by perfect peace and mutuality. When Jesus says, "I have come down from heaven, not to do my own will, but the will of him who sent me" (John 6:38), his point is not that God the Father calls the shots, and he, Jesus, is a lesser deity who just does as he is told. His point is that God the Father and God the Son are on the same page; they are a team; they've talked it over and made a plan. They have different parts to play—the Father sends, the Son is sent—but they are coauthors (with the Holy Spirit) of the drama.[9]

This, we think, is the kind of mutuality that husbands and wives should be striving for in their relationships with one another—not a pseudocooperation in which one spouse issues orders and the other hastens to comply, but a real cooperation in which there are real conversations and the kind of real give-and-take that is essential for true mutuality. This is surely closer to the mutual submission that is spoken of in Ephesians 5:21, and that is unpacked later in the chapter with words like *nourish, cherish, love* and *respect.*

Mutuality takes time. It takes effort. It takes a willingness to talk with one another and listen to one another, for long enough that it can become clear what the issues are, what the feelings and desires of both spouses are, and what some possible plans of action might be. Headship as decision making, by contrast, can seem quick and easy and far less personally demanding. Husband and wife don't really even have to work together: he just does his job and decides, she does her job and goes along, and they're done. And that is exactly the problem. They haven't actually dealt with their differences; they've just done an end run around them. They

---

[9]This is the conclusion reached by the Council of Nicaea in 325 and expressed in the Nicene Creed, a confessional statement accepted by all Christian communions since then.

are no more united when they are done than they were when they began. There has got to be a better way.

But before we talk about what a better way might be, we have to tell one more unpleasant truth about the control-and-acquiescence model of male-female relationships. Defining male headship as control and female submission as acquiescence is not just misguided; it is dangerous. By idealizing rigidly defined gender roles, assigning power in relationships disproportionately to men, and encouraging both men and women to see this as spiritually appropriate and desirable, a theological ideology for abuse in intimate relationships is set in place.

"My ex-boyfriend would always say to me that he was the one who should make all the decisions in the relationship, and that I should just follow him. That should have been the first warning sign to me, but it wasn't," wrote one woman. She was happy at first not to have to decide what movie they would see, but her boyfriend's controlling tactics rapidly escalated. So did his explosive anger.

One day, in the midst of a fight, she tried to leave the room. He slammed the door, grabbed her and pushed her against the wall. She tripped and fell. "He stood over me with his foot on my chest and said, 'Don't you ever try to walk away from me. No one would ever want you, anyway.' His words had no emotion in them. It was as if he had asked me to pass the salt at the dinner table. It was one of the most frightening moments of my life."

This woman was right: her boyfriend's explicit desire to make all the decisions in the relationship should have been a warning sign to her. Controlling behavior is a risk factor for abuse, and all the more so when it is gender-stereotyped and underwritten with Bible verses. Does this mean that all gender-stereotyped Christian relationships are abusive, or will inevitably become so? No, it does not. Most Christian men (and women) are not abusers. Most Christian relationships are not abusive, whatever ideas about relationships or gender roles the partners in those relationships subscribe to.[10]

But some relationships are abusive, and too often that abuse is overlooked, excused and justified on the basis of faulty ideologies of control. Not every child who plays with matches will set fire to the house. But we teach children not to play with matches, because even one house burnt down is one burnt-down house too many. Christians should encourage one another to reject theories of relationship that can function as risk factors for abuse, because even one abusive relationship is one too many.

Cooperation and Consensus

An alternative sometimes suggested to the headship-as-control model of marital relationships is egalitarianism, or the affirmation that husbands and wives should have equal regard for one another and an equal say in what happens in their marriage. The advantage of egalitarianism—and it is a considerable one—is that it avoids the pitfall of supposing that the deck should be stacked against one spouse from the outset, and instead encourages partners to encounter one another as equals.

It seems to us, however, that egalitarianism shares a major drawback with the headship-as-control model. Both of these views, as commonly construed, are much more about the distribution of power than they are about cooperation. The headship-as-control advocates want to see power concentrated in the hands of one spouse or one sex (the male). The egalitarians want to see power distributed evenly between both spouses and both sexes. But both too often see relationships between the sexes as a zero-sum game in which power held by one spouse can only come at

---

[10]For a discussion of family ideology in mainline and evangelical Christian churches, see W. Bradford Wilcox, *Soft Patriarchs, New Men: How Christianity Shapes Fathers and Husbands*, Morality and Society (Chicago: University of Chicago Press, 2004).

the expense of power held by the other. The egalitarians think power should be shared fifty-fifty; the headship-as-control party think the distribution should be, in one man's memorable phrase, "sixty-forty in favor of the guy."

Given the tendency on the part of all humans to hoard and mis-use power when that option is available to them, we think it is better to have power—including power in marriage—distributed broadly rather than concentrated narrowly. The mere distribution of power, however, does not in itself address the question of how true mutuality is to be fostered between spouses. How can hus-bands and wives learn, not just to compete with one another on a level playing field, but actually to cooperate with one another?

An image we have found helpful in envisioning what coopera-tion looks like is that of teamwork. When two people play on the same sports team, they are working together toward the same goal. They rely on each other's strengths and cover for each other's weaknesses. They pursue tactical strategies that benefit the team as a whole and set each other up to succeed. Most important of all, they practice and practice and practice, because any sport is the most fun when you play it well and often.

The same is true of relationships, and of the relational work (or play) that is involved in meeting the challenges posed by conflict within the relationship or by stressors outside the relationship. No one is born knowing how to handle stress or conflict. These are things we have to learn. We learn in our families, we learn in our childhood friendships, and we need to continue learning as we move into and through adult relationships like marriage.

Before you can learn to play a sport well, you need to know what counts as success. In basketball, success is a high score. In golf, success is a low score. In white-water canoeing, success is proceeding downstream right-side up. What is success where con-flict management in relationships is concerned? If a dating or engaged or married couple find themselves feeling irritated or down-right angry with one another, what will success in dealing with that conflict likely involve?

One thing it will not necessarily involve is making a decision. Many conflicts, perhaps even a majority of them, are not the kinds of things that can be resolved with decisions. Sometimes people get into arguments because they are tired and cranky. They don't need decisions; they need sleep. One woman recalled a late-night conversation she had with her fiancé. They were getting progressively more irritated with one another when they realized what was happening, called a timeout, and promised to revisit the subject the following day. "When the next day came, neither of us remembered what we were bickering over. It was just a conversation that was happening too late at night when we were both tired and vulnerable to fighting."

Sometimes the stressors are more significant than mere late-night crankiness. "I've noticed that my wife and I have been a bit short with each other recently," wrote a recently married man. "We seem to be walking on eggshells and taking offense very easily." What was making them feel so irritated? Once he'd thought to raise the question, it didn't take long to identify some likely reasons, among them too much work and too little money.

They didn't need to make decisions, either. They needed mutual understanding and compassion. They went out for ice cream and talked about how burdened they felt by their circumstances, and how frustrating it was not to feel supported by the other. The result? "We understand each other better and can relate to one another better. There are no more mystery arguments and hypersensitive spouses. When one of us does seem short or unreasonable, there is compassion instead of criticism."

Another set of conflicts that cannot be resolved with decisions are those that arise from differences in style or personality. Many relationships include one partner who likes to talk things over at greater length, and one partner who likes to deal with things more briefly and be done with them. Many relationships include one partner who thinks a conversation has been satisfying when he or she feels understood, and another partner who thinks a conversation has been satisfying when a problem has been solved.

It is easy for people with contrasting styles to drive each other crazy. It is harder—but ultimately far more rewarding—to learn to work together. An engaged woman recounted the story of a conversation she had with her fiancé. She had been feeling overwhelmed with balancing life, school and wedding planning. She wanted him to know how she was feeling, and maybe offer sympathy and a hug. He thought she wanted him to fix the situation. Why else would she bring it up? "When I told him there wasn't anything to fix, he got a little irritated with me. He felt like I had created an issue where there wasn't one."

In the past, situations like this had become arguments: he felt she'd picked a fight for no reason; she felt he didn't understand or care about her. This time, she took a deep breath, chose her words carefully, talked gently but directly about her own feelings, and listened patiently and receptively to what he said about his. "We discovered we both were feeling unimportant to the other. He felt I was putting the wedding before him; I felt he was making his friends the priority over me. We began to understand that we haven't really been on the same team recently."

They also realized that they wanted to be supportive of each other, and that by talking and listening to one another, they could be. "I was surprised at the successful outcome of this intense conversation, and am excited to make this kind of communication a habit," she wrote. It is exhilarating to discover that the two of you don't have to flee from conflict and will not be overwhelmed by it. You can wade into it, encountering one another in the real stuff of real life, and come out the other side knowing one another better, trusting one another more, and confident that you can do it again whenever circumstances require.

Sometimes, though, decisions do need to be made. If after a certain amount of discussion, a couple cannot agree, what should they do? Should they compromise? In theory, it sounds good: each one gives a little, each one gets a little, and everybody is happy. In practice, the more significant a decision is, the less amenable it may be to compromise. He's been offered a wonderful job, a thousand miles from all her family members. They can't compromise on half the job for him, or half the move for her. She longs for another child; he feels their personal and financial resources are stretched to the limit already. They can't compromise on half a baby.

And even if compromise is possible, it may serve more to escalate than to resolve the conflict. Consider, for example, the story told by one woman about her and her boyfriend's Christmas traditions. In her family, the habit of certain relatives was to give mountains of gifts to everyone, regardless of the givers' ability to pay for these gifts or whether the recipients needed or wanted them. In his family, Christmas was hardly observed at all: they gave no gifts, put up no tree, and viewed the whole season more as a hassle than as a celebration.

Suppose this couple were to go on to marry. What should they do about Christmas in their own family? Should they compromise, trying to cobble together a Christmas celebratory enough for her but not too much of a hassle for him? What exactly would such a compromise look like? And how quickly would it devolve into a yearly tug-of-war with both spouses frustrated and angry and counting the numbers of dollars spent and hours devoted (or not) to Christmas?

It is better, we think, to aim not at compromise but at consensus. Forming a consensus is something that many of us have had little practice in. Often we don't keep our friends long enough or relate to them deeply enough to have any need to work through disagreements with them. And our culture is so individualistic that it can be hard to imagine there can be a greater good than getting what I want, or at least as much of it as I can manage. But working with your partner to identify or create possibilities that will be positive for both of you can be far more satisfying than simply trying to split your differences.

Which is what this couple did. The first Christmas they were dating, she drew him aside and gave him the heads-up on her relatives' spending and giving habits, which she was actually quite uncomfortable with but had realized she could not change. He became angry; it sounded like she was bragging about everything her family did, particularly as it stood in such stark contrast to the lack of celebration in his own family.

As they talked, it became clear that there was more going on than her embarrassment and his anger. He had felt left out and upset all during his childhood when his friends would talk about their families' Christmas traditions or the gifts they had received. She, on the other hand, loved the warmth of many of her family's traditions and was frustrated only by what she saw as an excessive emphasis on gift giving.

> We talked about the way we would want to raise our family, and he was able to spend a few days with my family helping to pick out our tree, decorate and bake before he left to go home at the end of the semester. Together we were able to see that what we both wanted for our family was a Christ-centered Christmas and one that focused on traditions and time spent with family rather than how many gifts one could buy.

In the end, successful conflict management often is less about resolving conflict than it is about the process by which conflict is addressed. Some conflicts don't call for resolution, some cannot be resolved and others may resurface periodically over long stretches of time—perhaps even over the lifetime of the relationship. But that doesn't mean a couple has to be miserable or angry for all that time. Conflicts are like rapids on a river. If you and your partner have no idea how to navigate rapids, you might be terrified the first time you hit one. But once you have learned to run the rapids, navigating through them becomes a practiced routine. You might even come to enjoy the intensity of teamwork that running the rapids involves, even as you also enjoy the stretches of calm water in between.

In conflict management, as in any sport, there are rules to play by.[11] If something is bothering you, bring it up in conversation as gently as possible. If your partner brings something up, respond to him or her. If it's not a good time to talk, say so, and specify a better time, one not too far in the future. When that time arrives, keep your word and talk about it. Say what you think and how you feel, and give your partner time to do the same. When you're not talking, listen with all your attention to your partner. Take turns talking and listening until you both feel you have been heard and understood. Then—and only then—start strategizing about possible courses of action. Once you've identified some options, talk about what might work best for both of you. Take your time, trust the process and trust your partner.

As also in any sport, there are illegal moves to be avoided. Don't run away from talking about difficult things. Silence doesn't lead to peace; it only makes your partner frustrated and resentful. Don't devalue or dismiss your partner's feelings or concerns. They

---

[11]These rules are drawn in large part from Howard J. Markman, Scott M. Stanley and Susan L. Blumberg, *Fighting for Your Marriage: The Best-Selling Marriage Enhancement and Divorce Prevention Book*, new and rev. ed. (San Francisco: Jossey-Bass, 2001), pp. 183-202.

are just as valid as your own and deserve to be treated as such. Don't criticize your partner's character or motivation. A willingness to interpret each other's behavior in a positive light is essential if you are to learn to work together. Don't widen the scope of the conversation once you're engaged in it. One issue is enough to deal with at any one time. Don't let your own motivation be to win at any cost. Conflicts can be constructively resolved only when both parties desire a positive outcome for the other as well as for themselves.

Most importantly of all: treat one another with consideration and respect, all the time, no matter what. "In my relationship, I so quickly jump to teasing, criticizing, and just not really being all that nice," confessed one woman. "I think I do this because I view my fiancé as a 'safe' person whom I can be mean to, and have the confidence that love will still be there." But casual unkindness can do more damage than we realize. It corrodes the foundation of the relationship in ways that might at first be unseen, but that become all too apparent when difficult circumstances arise and the couple discover they have too small a store of mutual trust and respect upon which to draw in order to meet those challenges. Kindness counts, when you are dealing with conflict and when you aren't.

Dwelling in Safety

Peace and safety go together. A peaceful home is a safe home; a peaceful relationship is a safe relationship. The people of God have known this for thousands of years. As the psalmist sings, "In peace I will both lie down and sleep; for thou alone, O LORD, makest me dwell in safety" (Psalm 4:8).

If we are to be safe in our relationships with one another, we must learn to handle conflict wisely and well. This process almost always becomes more intense after a couple marries. "My wife and I never really needed good communication skills when we were dating," confessed one newly married man. "If we ever got mad at each other, all we had to do was spend a day apart from each other, and everything was fine. Once you're married, you can't do that."

Realizations like these can be unnerving. Did you really make a good choice in marrying one another? Can you really make it work? Of course it is a good idea to develop substantive conflict-resolution skills before you marry. But the real measure of strength, in an individual or in a relationship, is not whether you already possess given skills. The real measure of strength is whether, when it becomes apparent that those skills are needed, you can rise to the occasion and develop them.

By this measure, this young couple were doing just fine. They were finding the courage to be straightforward about their own feelings and frustrations and desires, and to listen nondefensively to one another. They were beginning to be able to perceive and to take responsibility for the ways that they themselves were contributing to the conflictual dynamics in their relationship. They were realizing how far they had to go in really knowing and caring for one another well.

They were also realizing how much power each of them had to avoid fanning the flames of an argument, and instead to say specific things that could make the other feel valued and respected and cared for, even in the midst of minor annoyances or major disagreements. And they were beginning to see that they could trust one another to be gentle and truthful and caring, even in the midst of those same annoyances or disagreements.

This couple was talking, they were listening, and they were growing in humility, confidence and security. These are all ways in which peace can take root and flourish in Christian relationships and in Christian homes and marriages. As we cultivate these qualities in our relationships, we increase the degree to which we can dwell in safety with one another.

5

Friendship

From Acquaintance to Intimacy

During much of the two-thousand-year history of the Christian church, marriage, love and friendship were thought of as quite different things. Marriage was a contract negotiated by the future bride's and groom's parents with an eye to the establishment of family alliances, the increase of the family fortune, and the production of heirs to that fortune. To love one's spouse was not against the rules, but love was neither the basis nor the point of marriage.[1] Many people found it simpler to look to marriage for heirs and elsewhere for love. And friendship was viewed as a separate entity entirely: a bond of intimacy shared not by partners bound to each other by a vow of marriage, but by free and equal individuals whose intimacy was based on common interests and mutual affection.[2]

---

[1]See, for example, Stephanie Coontz, "Historically Incorrect Canoodling," *New York Times*, February 14, 2005: "Christian veneration of married love is hard to discern in the first 1,500 years of church history. As one 12th-century authority wrote, no one 'disapproves' when 'a gentle and honest sentiment' softens the bonds of a marriage, but 'it is not the role of marriage to inspire such a feeling.' Similarly, it was not the role of such tender feelings to inspire marriage."

[2]See, for example, Gilbert C. Meilaender, *Friendship: A Study in Theological Ethics* (Notre Dame: University of Notre Dame Press, 1981).

Times have changed. For good or ill, most modern Americans—including most Christians—see marriage, love and friendship as things that ought properly to go together. A good marriage is a loving marriage, and a loving marriage is one in which spouses are attached to one another as friends. They like each other, they have fun together, they know each other well, they take pleasure in one another's company. A marriage in which there is no friendship cannot be a good marriage, in this view. There might be a kind of businesslike efficiency about it, but if there is no intimacy, no delight, no simple enjoyment of the other or pleasure in the relationship itself, then it is a sad and empty shadow of what a marriage ought to be.

As various historians and sociologists have pointed out, these greatly heightened expectations of marriage are directly related to the equally heightened instability of marriage in our day.[3] If you expect your spouse to be not just your economic partner and the other parent of your children but also the love of your life and your best friend, you have that many more opportunities for dissatisfaction and unhappiness, should any part of this scenario not pan out. And if economic and legal and sociological conditions permit you to exit an unsatisfying marriage via divorce, you may well find yourself contemplating this possibility. After all, doesn't God want people to be happy?

There are Christians who contribute to this destabilizing dynamic by emphasizing the all-encompassing bliss that, in their view, properly accompanies the married state. They laud marriage as the most intimate relationship anyone will ever have. Young people are counseled first and foremost to "marry your best friend." Husbands and wives are encouraged to guard the intimacy and privacy of their relationship by looking to each other

---

[3]This point is discussed at length by Stephanie Coontz, *Marriage: A History: How Love Conquered Marriage* (New York: Penguin, 2006).

alone for all fulfillment and happiness. And the result, too often, is not contentment but disappointment and disillusionment. It might be that a little more modest realism concerning the purposes and possibilities of marriage might go a long way toward helping husbands and wives build stable and satisfying relationships with one another.

At the same time, though, there is a lot to be said for the ideal of friendship within marriage. Who wouldn't prefer to be friends with his or her life partner? Working together in all of the tasks that life brings one's way is all very well, but wouldn't it be nice to find delight in and with each other along the way? Perhaps being more intentional about building friendship both before and within marriage can contribute to the effort to build stable and satisfying marriages. What is friendship, after all? What kinds of things keep people from learning to be friends with one another? And what choices and habits can contribute to the formation and deepening of friendship?

Affection and Eros

Friendship is a larger category than marriage. People can be friends and have friends long before they are in a position to marry, and indeed whether or not they ever marry. This ought to be good news—here, in friendship, is an opportunity for people to make the kinds of intimate and enjoyable connections with one another that can meet the need we all feel for substantive relationship with other members of the human community. And as an added bonus, we get to develop the skills that we will need to cultivate friendship with a future spouse, should we ever decide to marry.

Do we really take advantage of our opportunities for friendship? It would seem that they are numerous. Young people who grow up in the church are often members of youth groups that seem to supply them with dozens of friends. College students live in dormitories and attend classes and social events with hundreds of their fellow students. Teenagers and young adults are members of social-networking websites that allow them to number their "friends" by the thousands. But how well do we actually know any of these people? How well are we known by any of them?

Not very well, in many cases. Too often, what passes for friendship is a mile wide and a quarter of an inch deep. These relationships are, in fact, not friendships at all, but acquaintances—acquaintances whose superficiality goes largely unnoticed and unremarked, but acquaintances nonetheless. This reality was brought home to us in a particularly striking way during one of the first offerings of our course on Christian marriage. As an introduction to a conversation about families, we had asked our students to think of an event or time in the life of their family after which nothing was ever the same again.

In the ensuing discussion, several members of the class shared deeply personal stories from their families. One young woman talked about the death of her father from AIDS and the death a year later of an uncle, also from AIDS. Both deaths had taken place around Christmas time, and Christmas had never been the same since then. A young man talked about a brother who had been a very difficult child and adolescent, and whose relationship with their parents was severely strained as a result. Then the brother got his girlfriend pregnant. In the shock of this family emergency, a realization came to the parents: if we fail to support our son now, we will lose him forever. They sought help for themselves and for their son and his girlfriend, and this crisis proved to be a turning point in the life of the family. Things weren't perfect, but they were better. Another student talked about her father's struggles with alcohol and depression, and a suicide attempt that had reshaped the dynamic of her family.

The next week we received an essay from a woman in the class.

I have been a student at this institution for four years. I know almost every other member of this class. I have lived in the same dorm with many of them. I have eaten with them in the cafeteria. I have attended classes and worship services with them. It amazes me how much I don't know about them. These people are my classmates and friends, yet they are strangers. I never knew Katie's dad died of AIDS. I never knew Mark had a rebellious brother. I never knew Priscilla's dad almost committed suicide. I never knew.

This young woman certainly did not set out to be ignorant of some of the most formative experiences in the lives of those she counted as friends. And yet she was. Our sense is that she is not alone; that there are many, many people in the world who really don't know even the people they think of as their friends. Although there are a range of factors that contribute to this superficiality of relationship, one basic and widespread assumption is worth noting up front: the assumption that there really isn't any such thing as friendship apart from romance.

Affection and eros (sexual love) are not seen as loves that might be directed toward different people, with the result that you might or might not have a romantic partner but could still have one or more genuinely intimate friends. Instead, intimacy is assumed to be sexual by definition. If you want an intimate friend, you don't look for someone who is "just a friend." You look for a lover.

This conflation of affection and eros begins early on. Same-sex friendships in high school and college typically rank second in importance to romantic relationships. Where girls of an earlier generation longed for a "bosom friend"—that is, an intimate female friend—today's girls long for a boyfriend, and save their most intimate confidences for him. Boys, too, tend to be more eager to make time for girlfriends than for male friends. "It seems like I can never do anything with friends," sighed one unattached male. "All they want to do is be with that special someone."

Opposite-sex friendships, for their part, are simply assumed either to be overtly sexual or headed in that direction. One young woman explained,

> I got "the talk" in ninth grade from both my mother and my stepmother. Both almost expected me to lose my virginity by the time I was sixteen, because guess what—that's right around the time they lost theirs! So I am sitting there on the couch, and I am getting this talk about how I will most likely *not* save myself until marriage. It was like they were handing me a permission slip to have sex. I remember them saying things like, "We know how hard it gets," and "If you are going to have sex, let me know so we can prevent a pregnancy." I was mortified! I wasn't ready to have sex! I had a boyfriend at the time, but we were more worried about what time to meet for the movies than when and where we would do the deed.

These parents deserve credit for taking seriously the possibility that a fifteen-year-old might be inclined to have sex with her boyfriend. As they knew from experience, plenty of fifteen-year-olds do. But notice what they did not do: they did not engage their daughter in conversation about possible ways that her relationship with the boyfriend might become deeper or more mature without their having sex. Neither, apparently, did they broaden the conversation to consider how her relationships with anyone else might become deeper or more mature. Instead, they simply assumed that the intimacy of an opposite-sex friendship is or will be sexual, and the important thing is to ensure that no one gets pregnant.

Other adults are horrified at the prospect of teenage boyfriends and girlfriends having sex with one another, but they are not talking with young people about how they might develop nonsexual intimate relationships with their friends. They too assume that intimacy is by definition sexual, and they seem to hope that if you focus attention early enough and strongly enough on marriage, both intimacy and sex can be postponed until then. Fifteen-year-olds are slotted into Bible studies on the topic of "preparing for love and marriage." High school seniors are charged with planning their future weddings to as-yet-to-be-identified partners.

And "casual dating" is forbidden, on the assumption that casual dating is basically equivalent to casual sex. Teenagers are allowed to date only on the condition that they consider themselves as potential marriage partners, at which point the process is called "courting." "I once asked my high school Sunday school teacher how courting and dating differed," reported one woman. "She told me that girls who go on dates with boys they don't intend to marry usually end up having a lot of sex and getting pregnant."

The problem is that once you remove "casual dating" from the realm of licit relationships between persons of opposite sexes, you pretty much remove friendship too. Adults often assume that if two opposite-sex teens make plans to spend time together, then they must be dating, which is allowed only if they define themselves not as friends but as a potential married couple—despite the fact that they may be barely into their teens, and the chances that they will actually marry one another are vanishingly small.

As a result, many young people arrive on the brink of adulthood with very little sense that deep and lasting friendship is possible with anyone except with a spouse whom they have yet to meet. Their same-sex friendships have always been shallower than their romantic relationships, and instead of having built any lasting nonerotic relationships at all with members of the opposite sex, they leave behind a trail of rejects consisting of all the people they dated but ultimately concluded they could not marry.

This is a shame. Friendship is one of the great pleasures of life, regardless of one's romantic or marital status. It is possible to find intimate and rewarding friendship with persons of your own sex or, in somewhat different form, with persons of the opposite sex; but in either case, you are far more likely to find it if you look for it. Your middle school and high school years are not too early to start taking seriously the process of making friends and keeping them; your college and post-college years are not too late to begin the process if you did not do so before.

Adult friendship differs from more youthful friendship in its greater degree of focus on the challenges and rewards of the here and now. The friendship of young teenagers tends to include a fair amount of daydreaming about "when we grow up," the assumption being that one day this will just happen. As people arrive at adulthood, they realize that growing up happens gradually, and it never "just happens." Adult life must be made; it is not handed to you on a silver platter. The company of friends is a welcome element of adult life, as together you try to figure out who you are and where you are going and what it all means.

Adult friendship is also characterized, ideally, by a greater poise in navigating the sexual dimension of intimate relationship. Adolescent sexuality is a tumultuous experience for just about everybody, and it can seem that the easiest way to avoid sexual complications is to avoid intimacy. If you just don't get "too close," the thought is, you might be lonely but at least you'll be safe.

As you mature, however, it can become easier to recognize that friendships can be deeply intimate without being inappropriately sexual, and to make the kinds of choices that allow you to deepen friendships while remaining within the bounds of propriety. To the young adolescent, limits of any kind seem incompatible with intimacy. Becoming an adult involves a recognition that intimacy always exists within limits, and it brings an openness to identifying and living within appropriate limits for the sake of the relationship.

Affection and eros are not the same. A marriage, ideally, involves both. And even there, friendship will more likely grow and thrive if there is room made for bonds that are affectionate rather than explicitly erotic. It is easier to be friends, even with a lover, if you do not have to be lovers all of the time.

Obstacles to Friendship

So why aren't people better friends? The reasons go beyond the ideological privileging of eros over affection. There are practical obstacles to friendship too. People are busy. Their lives overflow with commitments of necessity and commitments of choice. Young adults are in school during the day and at work on the weekends, or else working during the day and going to school at night. They play sports or coach sports; they start new businesses; they volunteer with the youth group at church; they play in a band. In the midst of all this frantic activity, even boyfriends and girlfriends have a hard time making time for one another. "We are both so busy all the time," wrote one young woman. "We are chronic overcommitters to everything except each other."

Television is another obstacle to friendship. In many apartments and dormitory rooms, the television is on all the time. Whole relationships come to exist of little more than fighting over the remote. In the words of one woman: "He likes the sports channels. I like the girly channels. I like reality TV shows; he doesn't. He likes macho hunting shows; I don't. Cable makes our decisions harder, so we fight more. He usually wins." Other relationships are more peaceable; there aren't so many arguments about what to watch. But there's just as much watching, and just as little anything else. When do you talk if the television is on? Never, or only during commercial breaks. Either way, not much gets said or heard.

Electronic modes of communication pose another obstacle to genuine friendship. This may seem counterintuitive—shouldn't the ability to be in touch with anyone, anytime, lead people to be more connected with one another than ever? Well, they're connected, but too often not as friends. When people are together some of the time and apart at other times, friendship has an opportunity to develop between individuals who can choose really to make something of the time they have together. By contrast, nonstop text messaging and constant status updates on social-networking websites create the illusion of relationship between individuals who are never really apart and thus never really together, either. "I don't like being available 24/7 anymore," wrote one young man. "I want to be able to say, 'I'll see you later,' and actually mean *later*, not on Instant Messenger as soon as I get back to my place."

Electronic communication is problematic in other ways as well. When conversations take place face to face between particular individuals, both parties play a role in creating the interaction between them. Nonverbal cues like posture and facial expression assist people in deciding how much to say and how to say it, and whether and how to follow up on comments made by the other. None of that exists in electronic communication. Self-revelatory statements are made in isolation, and often to the world in general rather than to anyone in particular. They in turn are read by recipients who are busy with many other things or who may simply happen to be trolling the web for status updates. The result is less an electronic equivalent of conversation, and more a combination of exhibitionism and voyeurism.

People who have gotten used to playing the roles of exhibitionists and voyeurs often find it extraordinarily difficult to have actual conversations with people they actually know. It simply feels too risky. Sometimes they are willing to listen while others talk.

At other times, they don't want to hear others' concerns any more than they want to reveal their own. The result is relationships in which the participants "hang out" (or hook up), but exchange no personally identifying information. As one young woman wrote of herself and her ex-boyfriend, "I never knew what he was thinking or feeling, and I am pretty sure he had no clue what I was thinking or feeling." She found this frustrating and unsatisfying and ended the relationship, telling the boyfriend that she thought they should just be friends. Apparently it did not occur to her that perhaps the fundamental problem with the relationship was that they were not, in fact, friends. They were strangers.

We wonder about the extent to which these learned roles, and the superficiality and detachment that accompany them, feed into the use of pornography and porn-like materials among the young people who consume them. Pornography use is a complex phenomenon, and it is certainly not reducible to a single cause. But one of the great attractions of pornography is that it seems to offer the benefits of sex without the hassle of relationship. This is true both of the images, whether in print or online, that seem to be consumed mostly by men, and of the written material we have heard called "girl porn," namely magazines and romance novels, some of them primly chaste and others sex-saturated, but in either case holding out a vision of perfection that seems, like pornographic images, to offer everything and demand nothing.

Experiences with pornography vary. Many single men seem to see their porn use as, at best, a kind of stopgap measure, a way for them to deal with their sexual urges until such time as they can find satisfaction within an actual relationship. At worst, they are consumed with guilt and shame over what they experience as obsessive and addictive behavior that seems to affect everyone they know and that everyone seems equally helpless to stop. With women, the situation is somewhat different. Many Christian young people have been taught that single women have no sexual urges, so women who are reading sexually explicit magazines and books feel not only guilty and trapped but also profoundly isolated and abnormal. And the women who limit their reading to Christian romance novels, in which passion is awakened in the leading lady only after the ring is safely on her finger, often see these books as simple entertainment, even as they consume them obsessively.

The prospect of getting something for nothing has always been appealing, which is why pornography has been around forever. But pornography, in both its girl and guy varieties, holds a particularly straightforward and rational appeal for young people whose experience of relationality is ever more divorced from real interaction with real people. When an ever-increasing share of your communication takes place via various electronic media with people who are somewhere other than where you are and whose identities you may not even know, and when the role you play in communication is neither that of a fully focused speaker nor of an attentive listener but rather of an exhibitionist or a voyeur who can withdraw or turn away at any time, it only makes sense that sex should work the same way. The result is a further erosion of the ability of individuals to form genuinely intimate relationships—sexual or otherwise—with real people in real time and space.

This is the fundamental problem with pornography—not that it is about sex, but that it is, at base, not about sex at all. It is about a warped parody of sex, and thus about a warped parody of personhood and relationship. Pornography is not about building a relationship with a partner; it is about closing oneself off from relationship. Pornographic images convey domination and violence, not the openness and self-giving and mutual trust and trustworthiness that are essential to intimacy. And pornography is available at the click of a mouse, at any hour of the day or night. Compared with that, relationships with real people—whether friends or lovers—can come to seem impossibly inconvenient and tiresome.

Given the obstacles posed to the development of intimate relationships by the combined effects of factors like busyness, television, electronic communication and pornography, perhaps it is not surprising that people feel tempted to throw up their hands and look for ways to have relationships that do not require the tedious business of actually getting to know one another. One response to this impulse is books that purport to describe the supposedly fundamental differences between men and women, and advise the members of each sex on the proper care and feeding of the other sex.[4] Following these instructions is supposed to result in relationships that are easy rather than hard, and that are free of misunderstandings and hurt feelings.

It doesn't actually work. Yes, it is possible to make generalizations about men and women, and some such generalizations have merit. But generalizations tell you nothing about any particular man or woman. When people try to build relationships based on gender stereotypes, those stereotypes can easily be used as an excuse not to have to get to know one's partner. Instead of paying attention to one another and learning to talk or work together as the particular people they are, she just treats him as "a man" and he treats her as "a woman," and they develop no sense of one another as individuals or of their own relationship as arising out of the unique combination of their individualities. Whatever such a relationship is, it is not friendship.

A more spiritualized approach to doing an end run around the

---

[4]See, for example, John Gray, *Men Are from Mars, Women Are from Venus: A Practical Guide for Improving Communication and Getting What You Want in Your Relationships* (New York: HarperCollins, 1992). For an alternative perspective, see Deborah Cameron, *The Myth of Mars and Venus: Do Men and Women Really Speak Different Languages?* (New York: Oxford University Press, 2007).

trouble involved in getting to know another person is to suppose that the ideal Christian relationship has more to do with the relationship of each partner to God than it does with the relationship of partners to each other. The illustration typically given of this is of a triangle with God at the top and the relationship partners at the bottom two angles of the triangle. The idea is that as each partner moves closer to God, they automatically move closer to each other.

This doesn't work, either. While we in no way wish to suggest that the relationship of the individuals to God is unimportant or has no effect on their relationship to one another, human relationships cannot flourish unless the individuals involved go to the trouble of paying attention directly to one another. A heightened spirituality does not automatically confer greater knowledge of economics or geography or calculus, and it doesn't automatically confer greater knowledge of one's friends or one's spouse either.

Establishing Connections

If you and your partner want to establish and nurture a friendship that is truly intimate and satisfying, the most important thing you can do is to devote time to one another. This does not mean that the only people who can be friends are people with a great deal of leisure. It does mean that we need to be realistic about the number of commitments we can make while still nurturing our relationships with our friends, romantic partners or spouses. Many of us live in settings in which opportunities for interesting and worthwhile involvement exist in abundance. We could be engaged in a different recreational, volunteer or moneymaking enterprise every night of the week, and more on the weekends. We have to learn to say no to some of these possibilities so we can say yes to the things that are the most important, and to the people who are the most important.

This does not happen automatically just because people are married or romantically involved. Sometimes once a dating relationship is past the let's-spend-every-waking-moment-together phase, it enters the I-know-you'll-always-be-there-when-I'm-not-busy stage. The result is often a deterioration in the quality of friendship between the partners, either from simple neglect on the part of both of them, or because one partner resents the other's busyness and the busy partner resents the less busy partner's resentment.

Sometimes two busy partners become engaged and then married, hoping that once they are married they will be able to spend more time together. And sometimes that does happen. The season of engagement typically involves many unavoidable tasks, and once the wedding is over there can be more time to breathe and thus more time to focus on one another. But sometimes busyness is such a habit, and is so integral to each partner's sense of self, that marriage brings more, rather than less, busyness. When that happens, the friendship between newly married partners can run a very real risk of wilting like a tender seedling that no one has bothered to water.

So slow down. Do less, and be more intentional about it. Learn to gauge the fullness of your life, not by how madly you dash from place to place, but by how regularly you spend time with your partner. It may be that your life is truly unavoidably full of many necessary commitments. You may not always be able to spend long periods of time gazing dreamily into one another's eyes. But you can make choices that allow you to devote what time you have to one another and to nurturing your relationship in ways that deepen connectedness and mutual enjoyment.

You'll have an easier time doing this if you turn off the television. It's not that television is intrinsically bad—but television too easily becomes a default setting that crowds out any other form of activity. People sometimes interpret their television-watching habits as a function of busyness: when they get home after their long days, they are simply too tired to do anything else. But if you are genuinely too tired to do anything but watch television, then it may be that you are too tired to stay up watching TV. Go to bed, get some sleep, and maybe tomorrow you will have enough energy at the end of the day to talk with your mate over dinner, and afterward to take a walk or read a book or play a game. And maybe when the weekend comes, you will have enough energy to go to a park and throw a frisbee around, or visit someone who's sick, or do the food shopping together. A relationship that is built around activities like these will inevitably be far richer than one that is spent primarily in front of the television.

A second important element in establishing and maintaining friendship is conversation, and in particular the kind of conversation that we might call "friendship talk."[5] Friendship talk is not about managing the practicalities of everyday life—who is going to meet whom, at what time, and where; who is supposed to get the dog to the vet or put gas in the car. Friendship talk is also not about managing conflict—what are the issues, what are the partners' thoughts and feelings, what are the options. These kinds of talk are necessary, but they do not lie at the center of what most of us think of as friendship. Friendship talk is personal; it is fun; it can be serious or silly, as it takes us into one another's thoughts and memories, joys and sorrows, hopes and dreams. Without it, a relationship may be smoothly efficient, but it cannot really be called a friendship.

Friendship talk is most enjoyable, and most relationship nurturing, when partners feel safe enough to let down their guards and follow the thread of the conversation wherever it leads, trust-

---

[5]This phrase is used in Howard J. Markman, Scott M. Stanley and Susan L. Blumberg, *Fighting for Your Marriage*, 3rd ed. (San Francisco: Jossey-Bass, 2010), pp. 211-12 and elsewhere.

ing one another to speak frankly, listen compassionately and respond empathetically. This does not always come easily. "It seems obvious that Christians should be able to tell each other things so we can support each other," wrote one woman. "But we don't. If one person in your small group really opens up, everyone looks in the opposite direction and doesn't say anything. Why? Because we're scared."

It is scary to be trusted with another's personal self-disclosure. What if we don't know what to say? What if there is a problem we don't know how to fix? What if somebody starts to cry? And it is scary to be the one making the self-disclosure. Will we be judged? Will we be laughed at? Will our listener offer platitudes or quick fixes? Will he or she become uncomfortable and change the subject? The only way to find out is to give it a try. Start small, sharing things about yourself that you would like your friend to know, and asking your friend about him- or herself. If things go well, you can talk more and open up more and see what it looks like to develop trust in one another.

Where do appropriate boundaries in conversation lie? Individuals come into relationships with different ideas about this. Some people want to tell all and hear all, right now, or at least as soon as they have a ring on their finger. "There should be no secrets between spouses," wrote one individual. "How can you expect to be intimate with a person who does not share absolutely everything with you?" Other people are more inclined to hold back and to reveal their thoughts and feelings only slowly, if at all. "I think husbands and wives should be able to talk about anything, but I do not think that one spouse has the right to demand to know the other's secrets," wrote another.

Somehow, people of these different persuasions often manage to marry each other. They then have the opportunity to figure out how to balance self-revelation and discretion, inquiry and forbearance. The fact is, a person cannot possibly know "absolutely every-thing" about one's spouse or partner, and certainly not all at once. And it is never appropriate to demand to know anybody's secrets. But neither is it wise to put up a barricade labeled "my secrets" and hide behind it for the duration of your relationship. Husbands and wives, and boyfriends and girlfriends, owe one another both a certain amount of self-disclosure and a certain measure of pri-vacy. What exactly this looks like will depend on a lot of different factors, and it will almost certainly change over time as trust de-velops and deepens and the relationship matures.

A third element in building friendship has to do with the con-tent of friendship talk. You and your partner must be willing to learn to tell each other how you feel and what you want. There are few things that pose a greater barrier to intimacy than having no idea what is going on with your partner or what he or she wants or needs from you. One of the most counterproductive things you can do in a relationship, therefore, is to play a game we have come to call "Guess How I Feel."

As unpersuaded as we generally are by gender stereotypes, we have to concede that how people play "Guess How I Feel" does tend to fall out along gender lines. Some people (often men) grow up with little sense of their own feelings, or with not much expe-rience talking about feelings. When such a person plays "Guess How I Feel," he often has no idea himself how he feels, or if he does know, he is afraid to say it, for fear either of seeming un-manly or of starting a fight. It can take effort and intentionality for men to think about what they are feeling and, particularly if those feelings are negative, what might help them feel better. Then it takes more effort and intentionality to talk about it with their partner.

An engaged man once wrote an essay for us that nicely encap-sulated both the challenges and the rewards he had discovered in thinking about and expressing his feelings. He and his fiancée had spent a week vacationing at a beachside condominium with some other friends. They had had a wonderful time, but every time there was a lull in their schedule, they seemed to get into an argument. Why was this, he wondered? Finally he took some time to think about it. He was something of an introvert, he realized, and really wanted and needed some solitude every day. His fiancée, on the other hand, was more of an extrovert, and wanted nothing more than for the two of them to spend all of their time together. "At school the demands on our time are such that we have difficulty fulfilling our desires for either solitude or togetherness," he wrote. "Without saying it, we both brought our longings on vacation." Once he realized what was going on and was able to talk with his fiancée about it, she was able to give him some time to himself without feeling rejected, and they were able to enjoy their time together that much more, now that he wasn't so frazzled from having had no time alone.

Other people (often women) grow up encouraged to recognize in themselves a wide range of feelings and to talk about them freely, at least with same-sex friends. As a result, when women play "Guess How I Feel," they often know full well how they feel but want their partners to read their minds and give them what they want without their having to ask for it. "I am guilty of playing 'Guess How I Feel,' and am actually quite a pro at it," one woman wrote ruefully. A significant anniversary in her relationship with her husband had recently occurred. She had hoped that he would cook her a nice homemade dinner in celebration of the event. She didn't tell him this. He took her out to eat.

> Here is my point: I did not want to have to tell my husband that I hoped he would surprise me with a homemade meal. I wanted him to come up with the idea himself. That is what

would have made it meaningful for me. What is not meaningful is me saying, "You know, I really would like to have
you cook me a romantic dinner," and then having him cook
a nice dinner the next day.

What is going on here? Somehow the feeling is that if you get
what you want because you asked for it, it isn't worth as much as
if you got it without having to ask for it.

If I tell him what I would like and then he does it, I find myself thinking, "Well, I know why he did that—because I
asked him to!" It seems as if the action has been cheapened.
I want to be fair in my desires and expectations, but I also
don't want to puppeteer and always have to tell my partner
what I find touching or meaningful or thoughtful.

The only thing we can say to this is, if you tell your partner
what you want, and he gives it to you, that is good news! People
are not mind readers. Men in particular are not mind readers. The
same socialization that makes it hard for them to identify their
own feelings makes it that much harder for them to guess what
their partner's feelings might be. Give the guys a break, and tell
them what they can do to please you. It is possible that they may
be only too delighted to do it.

A fourth ingredient in building friendship follows from the last
one. It is important to do what lies in your power to please and
serve your partner, and to notice the things your partner does to
please and serve you. If you have been straightforward in communicating how you feel and what you want, your partner likely may
try to give you at least some of what you have asked for. One
woman told a story about her reluctance to open up to her boyfriend, whom she perceived as insensitive to her emotional needs.
The boyfriend, for his part, was frustrated that when he tried to
address her problems, she just got more upset. Finally it occurred

to her that she could tell him what she wanted: "When I am upset, I need you to listen and to say you are sorry that I am upset." To her surprise, it worked. "The next time I was upset, my boyfriend said to me, 'I'm sorry. You will be okay.' At first it seemed a little scripted, but he has gotten more creative with his sensitive statements since then. Now we laugh about how we both had misunderstood the other." We suspect that the boyfriend felt as empowered by these developments as she felt comforted by them. He had wanted all along to help her feel better. Now he knew what to do and was doing it, and she was noticing and appreciating it.

At other times, our partners may do things for us that we have not asked for and may not even realize we need. It is important to notice and appreciate these things too. Another woman told a story about various small thoughtful gifts she had given to her boyfriend, partly in the hope that he would take the hint and reciprocate. He did not. "You never do anything nice for me," she told him tearfully. "He responded by asking if I remembered how he had changed the oil in my car, and fixed the drain in my bathroom, and taken me to buy floor mats when I bought my new car. I guess because these were all things he did for me, rather than things he gave me, I hadn't realized the role they played in showing his care for me." This is one of the benefits of being in relationship with someone different from yourself—each of you is likely to have strengths and skills the other lacks, and when you care for one another in your own distinctive ways, both of your lives can be enriched.

Finally, friendship is nurtured when partners express their appreciation for one another. It is good to appreciate your partner; it is even better to say so, out loud. When she puts on her best dress to go out to dinner or to a party, don't tell her that she doesn't have to dress up for you; tell her how beautiful she looks in what she is wearing and how proud you are to be seen with her. When he is going out the door in the morning, don't just remind him to pick up milk on the way home; tell him how much you appreciate how hard he works and how good he is at what he does.

The expression of appreciation can be happy and positive. It can also be very intimate. A young man told a story about a surprise party he had given for his fiancée. "She leaned over during the party, kissed me, and said thank you. As little as that was, it meant the whole world to me." Later he realized he in turn needed to tell her how meaningful her words and gesture had been to him. "My revealing that to her was one of our most intimate moments together." Kindness builds upon itself, and as it does so, friendship deepens.

Choosing a Partner

The more attached to a friend you become, the more likely it is that you will begin to wonder whether it might make sense to choose this person as a marriage partner. But how do you decide? How can you discern whether this relationship has the potential to become a stable and satisfying marriage?

We have a few suggestions. First, consider your friend's character. Is this person kind? Is he or she honest? Does he or she consider the feelings of others? Can you trust this person to keep his or her word? Can you admire his or her behavior? If the answer to any of these questions is no, then this person is not marriage material. No one should marry anyone who is thoughtless, dishonest, untrustworthy, unkind or otherwise a person of poor character— not ever, not under any circumstances.

Second, consider how well you get along with your friend, and the extent to which you share his or her life goals. Do you enjoy one another's company? Do you want similar, or at least compatible, things out of life? Could you develop complementary careers? Can you see yourselves rearing children together? Can you live with one another's family circumstances? Are your faith commitments compatible? Can you make room for one another's weaknesses or shortcomings? If the answer to any of these questions is no, then marrying one another is probably not a good idea. You don't want to find yourself permanently at odds with your spouse, particularly on matters that you knew were an issue before you married.

Perhaps it seems that we should not have to make either of these points. After all, who would choose to marry a person of poor character? Who would choose to marry someone whose life goals they do not share, or with whom they cannot get along? Someone who is in love, that's who. We live in a culture in which the refrain, "But I love him (or her)!" is thought to trump every rational objection to a given match, and to be sufficient grounds to marry anyone, regardless of any other consideration. It's not true. Being in love is a fine thing, but you cannot marry someone just because you love him or her—not, that is, if you want to have any defensible hope that you will be able to build a flourishing and lasting marriage.

And finally, do not move in together, either as you are considering engagement or at any time before you are married. Seventy percent of American couples do cohabit before marrying, and many of them do so specifically because they believe premarital cohabitation will help them test the strength of their relationship and thus avoid divorce.[6] The objection raised most often to cohabitation by Christians—that it involves premarital sex and is therefore wrong—can seem pretty thin if cohabitation really does strengthen relationships.

In fact, it does not. Cohabitation—even with one's future spouse—is associated with an increased risk of breakup and di-

---

[6]David Popenoe, "The Top Ten Myths of Divorce," a publication of the National Marriage Project, Rutgers University (2002) <www.virginia.edu/marriageproject/pdfs/MythsDivorce.pdf>.

vorce, not a decreased risk. Cohabitation itself places stress on relationships. If you are cohabiting, you are not really committed to
each other, but not really *not* committed either, and that is a hard
balance to sustain. And it is precisely this lack of binding commitment to one another and to the relationship that makes cohabitation fundamentally different from marriage. Living together is not
a step in the direction of marriage; it is a step in a different direction. At best, it is irrelevant to your future marriage. At worst, it is
a risk factor for marital dissatisfaction and divorce.[7]

If you find yourself considering cohabitation, whether because
you can't afford two apartments or for any other reason, stop and
ask yourself: do you (both) want to be married, or not? If you want
to be married, you can be married for the cost of a marriage li-
cense. If you don't want to be married, don't muddy the waters by
moving in together. If you feel a need for more and better communication before making a decision about marriage, turn off the cell
phone and the computer and write letters, on paper, once or twice
a week for six months.[8] You are virtually certain to find your mind
considerably clarified at the end of that period, thus freeing you to
make an appropriate decision without the complicating and negative effects of cohabitation.

---

[7]Galena Rhoades, Scott Stanley, et al., in the *Journal of Family Psychology*, as reported
in "Unwed cohabiting couples 'risk divorce,'" *The Age*, July 15, 2009 <news.theage
.com.au/breaking-news-world/unwed-cohabiting-couples-risk-divorce-20090715-
dkfi.html>.

[8]For a lovely meditation on the superiority of letters to any other form of long-
distance communication, see Melissa Seligman, "One Husband, Two Kids, Three
Deployments," *New York Times*, May 24, 2009.

6

Sex

Embodied Communion

SEXUALITY IS AN INTRINSIC ASPECT of what it means to be a human being. People do not exist as androgynous, sexless beings. They exist as men and as women, bringing their gendered selves into every situation that they encounter. Men are men and women are women, not just in their romantic or marital relationships, but in all their relationships and throughout their lives. Sexuality is simply part of who people are; we can no more leave it behind or set it aside any more than we can leave behind or set aside our bodies themselves.

Sexual intimacy, on the other hand, is understood by Christians as appropriate only in certain settings and for certain purposes. Sex, marriage and children go together. Thus sex is appropriate only between spouses, and is meant always to be an expression of the intimate and self-giving bond that exists between husband and wife. Sometimes this may mean openness to procreation. It always excludes any domination over the spouse or any sexual use of the spouse that is abusive or purely self-serving. In sexual relations, spouses enact their marital promises with their bodies.

This is not natural. What comes naturally—at least to judge by how people actually behave—is a much more indiscriminant, self-centered and status-driven use of sex. People with power demand, or simply take, sex from people with less power. People have sex when they feel they want it or deserve it, with whoever happens to be handy. They find ways to have sex without relationship (via prostitution, hookups and pornography), sex without babies (via contraception), and babies without sex (via artificial reproductive technology).

Christian sexual morality, in other words, is a divine possibility if it is a possibility at all. There is an obvious biological connection between sex and babies, but it turns out that that is nothing modern science can't get around. And there is nothing obvious or biological about the restriction of sex to marriage. Christians locate sex within marriage, not because it is natural to do so, but because Christian marriage reflects God's covenantal and creative relationship with his people, and sexual relations are a sign and seal of that covenantal relationship between spouses.

Christian convictions about the unique appropriateness of marriage as a context for sexual relations, combined with the simple reality of the gendered bodies and selves that humans take with them everywhere they go, present the church with both an opportunity and an imperative: to shape the characters and the habits of Christian young people (and older people) in ways that allow us all to grow into a mature sense of ourselves as men and women, and (if we marry) as husbands and wives who can give ourselves to one another fully and freely as sexual partners.

Does this actually happen? Not as often as it should, and never automatically. The truth is that sex is complicated and often confusing. Parents and other adults do not always guide the church's children well. Young people too often receive misinformation or bad advice, or are simply left to figure it out themselves. Those young people then grow into older people who find themselves with few resources for navigating adult life and adult sexuality.

How exactly are Christian young people formed sexually? What are they taught to do and to expect from themselves and from others, as adolescents, as single adults, as married men and women? And what might be some helpful ways that all of us as Christians might think and act with respect to sex and sexuality, whether we are single or married?

Sexual Formation

If sexual relations are appropriate only to marriage, are single people, of whatever age, even allowed to think about sex or to experience themselves as sexual beings? Most of our students have been given an answer to this question long before they arrive in our classroom. That answer is, "No!" Sometimes the no is conveyed through silence. "In guidance class at my Christian high school we covered every subject except sex," wrote one woman. "It was always assumed that Christians should stay celibate until marriage, so there was nothing to discuss." "I never had a sex talk with my parents," wrote a young man. "Public-school sex education stepped in to give me the cold mechanics. But that's all they were authorized to give. Had it not been for that, my only education would have been pornography, the stories of my peers and my own experience."

At other times the no is made explicit, usually in the form of warnings about premarital sex, which is typically portrayed as uniquely and unspeakably awful. "I was taught that sex before marriage was pretty much the worst possible thing you could do," wrote one young woman. "I mean, we were taught that murder was very wrong, but obviously we would never do that, so sex before marriage was probably the worst thing we could ever do."

Corresponding to premarital sex as the worst possible sin, "purity" is presented as the most fundamental virtue. Christian young people are taught that "any touch is too much." They are encouraged to wear purity rings that symbolize their resolution to remain virginal until marriage, and encouraged to postpone their first kiss until marriage as well. They attend youth group conferences at which the speakers portray virginity until marriage as the greatest of all goods, and weddings at which the purported purity of the bridal couple is the primary focus of the ceremony.

The primary weapon in the war against premarital sex appears to be fear. "My Christian friends and I were never exactly sure what it was we were to fear about premarital sex," wrote a young man. "All we knew was that it was awful—not quite a fate worse than death, but clearly a close second." Another man explained,

> Two main things about sex were communicated to me in my high school years. First, if you do it you will feel guilty beyond measure. Second, either you will get a girl pregnant or you will contract a disease. Either way, the motivation for not having sex was not love for God, or a desire to follow Jesus or accurately to reflect the image of God, or anything positive at all. It was fear.

Shame is another frequently deployed weapon. A young woman told this story:

> Every year my youth group held a "True Love Waits" weekend. One year, when I was about fifteen years old, my youth leader used a plate of cookies to make a point. All of the cookies were huge and absolutely delicious, until we got to the very last cookie. It was much smaller, a little burnt, and had a bite taken out of it. My youth leader told us that once you have had sex you are like the bitten cookie, and you will be left at the bottom of the plate. By that time, I was no longer a virgin. I knew I was a bitten cookie—that no good man would want me, and that God would not want me either.

Do these tactics work? Well, they certainly do produce Christian youth who are ignorant, afraid and ashamed. Many of these same young people are also cynical, resentful and isolated. They are cynical because they have discovered that their parents and churches have lied to them about the risks and results of premarital sex. They have been told, for example, that sexual sin results inevitably in guilt, pregnancy and disease. When they try it for themselves, they find they enjoy sex, and that safe sex can be pretty safe, after all. Then they wonder: is anything they have been taught true? Or is it all lies?

Young people resent being lied to. One young woman wrote,

> I feel betrayed that my parents and my church did not respect me enough to tell me the truth. Did they really think that I would break the rules they had set for me if I found out I might not regret premarital sex at first? Or that women really want sex more than Christians say they do? Or that bodies are really not so bad after all? I found out the truth eventually, but I wish I could have found it out from my parents and my church, and not from the popular media.

And they feel profoundly isolated in their efforts to navigate their emerging sexuality. "The manner in which I was to deal with raging temptation (a subject my generation's parents were never very open or honest with us about) was left completely up to me," wrote one young man. He continued,

> Looking back, it felt like all we got was a healthy serving of 1 Corinthians 10:13 ("No temptation has overtaken you that is not common to [everyone]") with a side of Philippians 4:13 ("I can do all things in him who strengthens me"). Armed with these Bible verses and a tragically oversimplified understanding of love and sex, I don't think it's a stretch to say I was ill-equipped to figure out my sexuality.

Even the children of well-intentioned parents find themselves without much guidance.

My mom is one of the most amazing moms out there. She has tried her very best to instill good morals and values in her children. But after having had a boyfriend, and now being engaged, I cannot help but wonder why she did not talk to me more about sex. I feel like she hid the truth from me. I never knew that I would want sex so much. I never knew that I would struggle with purity and chastity as much as I do. Why did she not tell me this?

When young people make poor choices, their isolation increases. "After I had sex, I really did not feel like I could go to anyone in my church to talk about it," wrote a young man. "I felt like I did not have a safe place to talk about what had happened." Another person described a conversation she had with her mother about a sermon they had heard on sex and singleness that had emphasized the woeful condition of those (presumably outside their circle of acquaintance) who had had premarital sex. "It was all I could do not to start crying. We were not talking about some distant person, some heathen. No, we were talking about me."

What happens when people who have been formed in these ways approach marriage? In place of the fantasy of "purity," there is often the reality of sexual experience to be reckoned with. Christian rhetoric about virginity as the most desirable characteristic in a marriage partner can cause real despair in people whose virginity was taken from them violently, as victims of rape or childhood sexual abuse. "I do not feel like I am good enough for the type of man I want to marry," wrote one such woman, speaking not only for herself but for many other survivors of sexual violence.

Those who gave their virginity willingly are often not proud of their behavior after the fact, and wonder what this means for their marriage prospects. "I'm scared of telling a future boyfriend about the mistakes I've made in the past," wrote another young woman. "Will he still want me if he knows I'm not pure?" Men have similar worries. One told us of a recurrent waking nightmare of his, in which the girl of his dreams looked into his eyes and said, "I've saved myself for you," and he had to reply, "Well, um, I didn't save myself for you."

A rhetorical move made by some Christians at this juncture is to talk about the possibility of a "reclaimed" or "renewed" or "recycled" virginity for those who have committed sexual sin prior to marriage. There are real problems with this language. What gets recycled? Garbage! And that is exactly what a lot of young people who have made poor sexual decisions believe themselves to be. The language of renewed virginity also implies that a person who has had sex before marriage needs to "go back" and be a virgin again, any sort of virgin. But you can't go back. Nobody ever gets to go back. All you can do—all anyone can do—is go on, go forward, and do better next time. But is that good enough, where virginity and sexual experience are concerned?

Another feature of the sexual formation received by many Christian young people is an emphasis on the overwhelmingly satisfying sex they will certainly have as soon as they marry. "I think a lot of Christian guys expect a couple-year-long orgiastic explosion after getting married," wrote one young man. As comic as it might seem, this expectation is actively encouraged by at least some in the abstinence-before-marriage industry: fabulous sex on your wedding night and every night thereafter is the reward promised to those who save themselves for marriage.[1]

Does it really work this way? Well, no. One young woman wrote the following:

---

[1]Motoko Rich, "A Writer's Search for the Sex in Abstinence," *New York Times*, October 14, 2007.

I and a number of my recently married friends all saved sex for marriage. Every one of us has the same opinion: sex after marriage is not at all what people make it out to be. We were all led to believe that if you remained abstinent before marriage, there would be a huge reward waiting for you in the bedroom once you got married. You would have an instantaneously pleasurable and "successful" sex life. The wedding night would be the most amazing night of your life, and if it wasn't, the only reason could be that there was something wrong with you or with your relationship. Let's be realistic: this is a myth.

What if you don't save yourself for marriage? That is complicated too. Couples who initiate their sexual relationships before marriage often find themselves navigating a complex mix of emotions about their premarital sexual involvement: guilt (because they believe they should have waited), anger (at themselves for having transgressed boundaries they had promised each other they would not), embarrassment (at not being as pure as they are probably hoping their friends and family believe they are) and disappointment (at not being able to look forward to the wedding night as their first time). Christian sexual formation offers little to help them make sense of all of this.

On the subject of marital sex beyond the wedding night, the sex education received by most Christian young people falls completely silent. The assumption seems to be that if the bride and groom can be brought safely virgin to the altar, then married sex will just take care of itself. If they're not virgins, it's their tough luck. And in any case, there is really nothing to say. There is nothing to be said about married sex to the unmarried, because it might put ideas into their heads. And there is nothing to be said about married sex to the married, because once the ring is on your finger, sex comes perfectly naturally—right?

Sex and Singleness

It is not possible to put ideas into the heads of single people by talking about sex with them. Those ideas are already there. They have been there since the onset of puberty, and they intensify as young people enter into serious relationships and begin to contemplate marriage. "I can envision having sex with my girlfriend just as I can envision us doing all the other things married couples do," wrote a young man. "This is a time in which I really need all the guidance I can get, because the conversation about sex changes on a fundamental level when marriage is clearly on the horizon." Part of honoring people as embodied and therefore sexual beings is being willing to talk about sexual matters openly and honestly, whether we are single or married.

One of the first things to be said about sex is that it is okay not to know everything. Our culture glorifies sex and sexual prowess—many people simply assume that sexual experience and personal maturity go together, and that anyone who is virginal or otherwise inexperienced is for that reason a mere child. Children themselves think this, and flaunt whatever degree of sexual experience they have as evidence of their supposed maturity. Experienced boys (or boys pretending to be experienced) lord it over other boys; experienced girls condescend to girls reputed for their innocence or modesty: "You're better off as you are; after all, one thing does lead to another."

In reality, experience and maturity are not the same thing. It is possible to have a great deal of sexual experience and to be a thoroughly immature person, and possible likewise to have little or no experience of sexual relationship and yet to be secure and well-grounded in one's own masculinity or femininity. What that security and well-groundedness look like may vary from person to person. You may be content to leave sex as a mystery to be solved by marriage, and to devote most of your energy as a single person to thinking of other things. Alternatively, you may be much more actively curious, and may really benefit from conversation with friends or from books that may address some of your questions. And there is nothing wrong with being curious! Sex is interesting; there is no reason not to think about it and talk about it.

While there is far more to sex and sexuality than decisions whether to have sexual relations with a given person, decisions like these do loom large in the experience of many single people. We have found it helpful to make a distinction between premarital sex properly so-called, and sex that is simply nonmarital. Non-marital sex does not involve two people who are on their way to the altar with one another but just haven't gotten there yet. On the contrary, it involves people who have no intention of marrying one another, but who are having sex with one another anyway for any of a variety of reasons. Girls have sex with guys because they know that is what is expected of them. Guys have sex with girls because that's what they want and they know how to get it. Both men and women have sex because they think everyone else is doing it, and they want in. They have sex because they think it is no big deal, or because they are "in love" and sex seems like the obvious next step.

Nonmarital sex is a bad idea. Sex is meant to be an intimate communion between partners who are vowed to each other. Sexual relations are meant to express mutual consecration: "I give myself to you, and you give yourself to me." When partners who are not married to each other engage in sexual relations, they tell a lie with their bodies. Lies hurt people, whether or not they realize it. Some damage is obvious—sexually transmitted disease (which does really happen, just not all the time), or betrayal by a partner who you thought cared for you but who turns out simply to have been using you.

Some damage is less obvious. It is very difficult to form a well-grounded sense of one's own self, or to lay secure foundations for relationship, in the midst of the promiscuous sexual behavior that marks too much of the young-adult social scene. It is similarly difficult to make a well-considered decision about marriage with a person with whom you are already having sex. The sexual relationship can make it seem as if, for all intents and purposes, you already are married—so what's to decide?

And some damage can involve innocent third parties, namely, babies conceived by people who cannot possibly parent them adequately, or who for one reason or another are unable or unwilling even to bring those children into the world. The fact is that sex tends to lead to babies. This reality is often obscured in the contraceptive world we live in, but we forget it at our peril.

Hence a guideline that we offer our students as a reference point for sexual decision making: Never have sex with anyone with whom you would not wish to raise a child. The reasoning behind the guideline is this: the rule that many Christian young people are most familiar with (no sex except with your spouse) can seem purely formal. It sounds like you have to have a permission slip in order to have sex, and the only reason you have to have the permission slip is because somebody—God, the Bible, the church—says so. Even when young people abide by this rule (and more than a few of them do), they often find it hard to explain to themselves or to others why they are doing so. It seems arbitrary, and it seems childish—what other things in their lives do they do just because someone says so?

In contrast to this, stating the criterion for sexual decision making in terms of childbearing and child rearing shines a light on the nature of sexual activity itself. Sex is so powerful and person-centered an activity that by its very nature it can and often does result in new life. Pregnancy is not a "risk"; pregnancy is one of the things that sex is for. For this reason, even if you take steps to see that no new life results from your sexual activity—that is, even if you contracept or engage in nonprocreative sexual activity—sex is still something you should share only with someone with whom you would be willing to create and receive a new life.

What, then, about genuinely premarital sex? By this we mean sexual relations between partners who have made a promise of marriage to each other, who have told their parents and set a date, and who have been unable to contain themselves until after their walk down the aisle. There are three things to be said about this.

First, premarital sex is very common, and always has been. In agrarian societies like those of the Middle Ages, when families depended on children for labor, premarital pregnancy was seen as a kind of insurance policy, allowing couples to know before marriage that their union was fertile.[2] Records of marriages and births in eighteenth- and nineteenth-century America show that a large proportion of children were born to parents who either were not legally married at all, or who had married fewer than nine months before the birth of the child.[3] Closer to our own time, an analysis of data gathered between 1982 and 2002 has shown that by age twenty, about 75 percent of Americans have had premarital sex, and by age forty-four, 95 percent have done so.[4]

There has simply never been a golden age of chastity, in which all brides deserved to wear white because they were all virgin. Many, many brides and grooms, throughout the history of the

---

[2]Stephanie Coontz, "The Heterosexual Revolution," New York Times, July 5, 2005.

[3]Stephanie Coontz, "Op-Chart: A Pop Quiz on Marriage," New York Times, February 19, 2006.

[4]Lawrence B. Finer, "Trends in Premarital Sex in the United States, 1954-2003." Research sponsored by The Guttmacher Institute, published in Public Health Reports 122 (January/February 2007). This study defines "premarital sex" as "either having had vaginal intercourse before first marrying or ever having had intercourse and never having married." It thus does not make our distinction between "nonmarital" and "genuinely premarital" sex but rather defines any sex before marriage as "premarital."

world and the history of the church, have been sexually experienced, often with each other, before they got to the altar. Premarital virginity is a good thing, and there are good reasons, both theological and practical, to hold it up as an ideal and strive for it in practice. But it is not and has never been the norm, in the sense of being the actual experience of most individuals or couples.

Second, premarital sex is not the worst thing anybody ever did. We do not say this with the intention of giving anyone permission to have premarital sex. We say it in an effort to introduce some perspective and a sense of proportion to the conversation. When we talk about this in class, we tell a story that we read somewhere, in a now-forgotten source, of a person who was a spiritual director for men aspiring to join the Orthodox priesthood. These young men often turned their conversations with him into long recitations of sexual sin. It got rather tedious, the spiritual director acknowledged with a sigh, but he was thankful for it nonetheless, because if it hadn't been for sex, these young men would have had no sense of sin at all.

Our classroom always fills with self-conscious laughter at this point. If it weren't for sex, many of our students would have no sense of sin either. We have received many essays from young people who confess deep regret and a sense of alienation from God as a result of some aspect or other of their sexual behavior. Hardly ever do we receive an essay confessing similarly deep regret or alienation as a result of anything else. Gluttony, avarice, sloth, envy, anger, pride—so far as we can tell, many Christian young people have hardly heard of the other six deadly sins.[5] For most of

---

[5]For an interesting treatment of these, see Dorothy Sayers, "The Other Six Deadly Sins," in *The Whimsical Christian* (New York: Collier, 1987); originally published in *Unpopular Opinions: Twenty-One Essays* (London: Victor Gollancz, 1946). As Sayers points out, lust has traditionally been seen as the least serious (precisely because it is the most "fleshly") of the seven deadly sins, and yet today it seems to be the only sin many people can identify as sin.

them, sin is lust, or the things that lead to, follow from or accompany lust, almost by definition.

Along with this near-identification of sin with sexual misbehavior goes a curious mix of antinomianism and legalism. To whatever small extent Christian young people are aware of other sorts of sin in their lives, they seem to assume that they needn't bother much about it. After all, they have been saved by grace, and neither God nor other humans are going to hold their sin against them. But to whatever extent they perceive sexual sin in their lives, to that extent they find themselves fearing that they will never be able to restore their relationships with God (who seems impossibly distant and crushingly disappointed in them), with other Christians (who expect good behavior from their fellow Christians) or with non-Christians (who will never be able to take seriously the witness of Christians who are sinners).

We wonder if it might be as well for many Christians to ease up a little on the sexual side of things, and to take many other things much more seriously. There can be, to be sure, particularly life-changing consequences to sexual sin, and particularly sharp regrets that accompany it. But a true appreciation of the nature of grace can help us put things in perspective, seeing sexual sin as neither more nor less significant than other kinds of human failure, and helping us to reach out for forgiveness and to grow in holiness, whatever our circumstances.

The third thing to be said about premarital sex is that it is better avoided, and this for several reasons. In the first place, people can easily fool themselves, or someone else, about intentions to marry. "I felt so bonded to my boyfriend at the time," one young woman wrote. "We had been together for almost three years. We both thought we were going to marry each other, and this is how we justified sleeping together. It didn't seem wrong at all. And then we broke up. That's when I realized the mistake I had made."

In the second place, if you believe sex before marriage is wrong but you are doing it anyway, you are going against conscience, and this is never a good idea. To do that which you believe to be wrong damages your conscience; it makes it harder to care about the difference between right and wrong and to choose the good and reject the bad. And where sex in particular is concerned, engaging in sexual activity that you believe to be wrong can entangle guilt with sex in a way that can be difficult to undo later.

And in the third place, what if a baby is conceived? "My freshman year roommate left school and got engaged," wrote another woman. "She had sex with her fiancé, thinking they were going to get married. Then she got pregnant, and he got freaked and canceled the engagement. If that isn't a reason not to have sex with the person you're engaged to, I don't know what is."

The fact is that we live in the midst of a secular culture that too often sees babies conceived by young people as an intolerable burden, and a Christian culture that too often sees babies conceived by unmarried people as evidence of unforgivable sin. If one of you becomes pregnant before you are married, will you and your partner have the moral courage and the practical support necessary to go ahead and marry one another—perhaps sooner than you'd planned—and form a family into which to welcome your child thankfully and without resentment? Think about it carefully; talk with each other about it, and make your decisions accordingly.

Sex and Marriage

"My husband and I have an ongoing debate about sex," wrote one young woman. "Does more sex lead to greater intimacy, or does greater intimacy lead to more sex?" Their sense was, it works both ways. Sex is about relationship. A satisfying intimate relationship outside the bedroom helps make a satisfying sexual relationship possible. And a satisfying sexual relationship buoys and enhances a couple's relationship as a whole.

The foundations for a positive marital sexual relationship begin to be built long before the wedding night. If you and your partner are cultivating an intimate friendship in which you can enjoy one another playfully, talk with one another openly, work on shared projects cooperatively, problem-solve constructively, and relax together trustingly, you are well on your way to building a relationship in which sex can play a positive and intimate part.

It is a good idea to be talking about sex itself both before and after the wedding. Everyone has a sexual self that he or she brings into relationship. Part of getting to know your partner, and of being known by him or her, is sharing that sexual self with your partner. When and how did you first begin to be aware of yourself as a sexual person? What have you been taught—whether by word or by example—about sex by your parents or other important people in your life? What have your own sexual experiences been? Have those experiences been positive? Negative? Confusing? Traumatic?

It may not be important to share all the gory details. In fact, if there are a lot of gory details, it may be as well to draw a veil decently over some of them. But it is always important to be honest with yourself and with your partner about who you are, where you have been and whether you are prepared to bind yourself to the disciplines of sexual exclusivity and faithfulness that Christian marriage requires, and to open yourself to the sexual intimacy and vulnerability that Christian marriage can make possible.

Many people have fears or worries about sex, particularly if they are sexually inexperienced and are approaching marriage. Men may worry that on the wedding night, they will not know what to do. Women sometimes worry that they will not like sex, or that it will hurt them. Voicing any fears to one another can help you both relax and realize that together you can figure it out. "We talked a lot during sex," reported one recent bride. "At first we didn't know what we were doing, or if we were doing it right. We would crack up laughing because we felt like little kids. It was great to be able to talk about that and laugh together so neither of us had to feel awkward alone."

Another common set of fears involves making what we have heard called the transition from "No, no, no!" to "Yes, yes, yes!" The sexual formation of many Christian young people includes heavy doses of guilt that are meant to keep them out of trouble. The result often is a sense that sex itself is bad. "My entire existence as a Christian has been based on the idea that sex is bad and I should not place myself in any situation that might become compromising," wrote one woman. "This has made me very fearful of and anxious about sex. I am afraid that when I finally am 'allowed' to have sex I will either be too afraid to go through with it, or I will feel guilty or dirty because I finally have."

This is a very unfair burden to place on anyone. The truth is that sex is not bad. The truth is that sex is powerful, and like anything powerful, it is dangerous if misused. A right use of sex requires discipline and wisdom, which is not at all the same as terrified avoidance. It might thus be better to think of the transition from singleness to marriage not so much as a transition from no to yes, than as a transition from one kind of discipline to another.

The discipline of singleness requires us to be men and women in relationships in which sexual energies are sublimated rather than expressed directly.[6] The discipline of marriage offers us the opportunity to cultivate sexual intimacy with a spouse. Either way, sex is not framed as bad one day and good the next, but as a dimension of human existence that is appropriately lived out in

---

[6]For a discussion of the distinction between sublimation and repression, see Kathleen Norris, *The Cloister Walk* (New York: Riverhead, 1996), p. 260.

different ways depending on one's circumstances.

Even if you have been encouraged—inadvertently or intention-ally—to view sex with fear or guilt, it is possible, with patience and gentleness, to make the transition to married life and married sexuality in a way that is positive and life-giving. One woman told the story of a friend who had been "scared to death" about the prospect of sex. "I talked to my friend after she was married. She told me that she loves sex and I should never let anyone tell me it isn't beautiful and fun. What a relief!"

There are multiple dimensions to sexual relationship. Tradi-tionally, Christians have summed up the purposes of sex in two categories: the unitive and the procreative. This is fine for short-hand, but can use some unpacking. Sex is about more than the simple union of bodies, with or without pregnancy as a result. Sex involves the giving and receiving of pleasure. It involves sharing emotional and physical intimacy. It gives us a way to connect and reconnect in the midst of the stresses and strains of everyday life. It allows us to feel desirable and desired.

Sex, thus understood, is more than intercourse. Sex is an inti-mate, erotic way of relating to one another in and through our bodies. Sex involves affection, sensuality and playfulness. It in-volves an erotic response to your partner and to his or her erotic response to you. It involves a satisfaction that is grounded in shared enjoyment of sensual and sexual pleasure, whether or not a given sexual encounter involves either intercourse or orgasm.

This kind of expansive and flexible understanding of married sexuality runs strongly counter to some common habits of thought and behavior. In particular, it contrasts with the inclination to equate sex with intercourse. This inclination begins long before marriage. Many Christian young people grow up pressed on one side by an intensely sexualized secular youth culture in which just about anything goes, and on the other by an intensely moralistic

Christian youth culture in which virginity is prized above all else. In such a context it can seem to make sense to characterize any and all sexual behavior other than vaginal intercourse as "not really sex." This opens the door for Christians to be almost as promiscuous as their non-Christian counterparts, since as long as they avoid "the act," they can claim still to be virgins.

It is hard to know how much of this reasoning is a reflection of genuine confusion and naiveté, and how much of it is more or less calculated hypocrisy and self-deception. But the damage done by such attitudes is not limited to single people. These attitudes carry through into marriage, where sex continues to be understood in very reductionistic terms, as neither more nor less than intercourse. When sex equals intercourse, it very easily turns into a performance. No sensual or erotic scenario that does not culminate in intercourse and orgasm counts as sex, and no such scenario can be experienced as satisfying.

This might not seem like such a problem when partners are young and the physical mechanisms underlying arousal, intercourse and orgasm tend to function more or less automatically. But as people get older, sexual function—particularly for men—becomes less and less automatic. So what do you do, once your body no longer behaves like the body of an adolescent? If you have defined sex as intercourse, and graded it pass-fail, you may not see any good options. You may end up deciding you would rather not have sex at all than try to have sex and fail.

Indeed, this often happens. Some two-thirds of couples have ceased to be sexual by sometime in midlife. In the vast majority of cases, the decision to do this is made unilaterally and silently by the husband, who so fears sexual "failure" that he would rather avoid being sexual at all.[7] Because there has been no conversation

---

[7]Michael Metz and Barry McCarthy, "Eros and Aging: Is Good Enough Sex Right for You?" *Psychotherapy Networker* (July/August 2008) <http://psychotherapynetworker.org>.

about this, wives have no idea what the problem is and can easily conclude they are no longer attractive to their husbands. And the marriage as a whole becomes less intimate and less satisfying.

Perhaps it seems premature to be talking about such things in a book addressed to young people, many of whom aren't even married yet. But a fear we have heard voiced again and again, by both men and women, is that their marriages will become cold and sexless as they get older. It is extremely difficult for many young people to imagine how their parents ever managed to conceive their children, because it does not appear that the parents have any current physical relationship whatever. Is this inevitable? Is sex a fire that burns brightly in youth and flickers out by middle age?

It does not have to be this way. Bodies change over time, and sex changes over time too. But that change does not have to be from good to bad—it can be from the goodness of youth to the goodness of maturity. Sex is not just a matter of plumbing and hormones. Sex is about relationship and vulnerability and openness to intimacy. These aspects of marriage only get better with age, and as a result, more mature couples can find their sexual satisfaction increasing as the years go by.

There are things you can do while you are young to help this happen. The single most important of these things is to recognize that in sex as in so many other things, the perfect is the enemy of the good. From Hollywood movies to porn videos to television and print advertising, we are surrounded by images of "perfect" sex, which always involves people with perfect bodies in romantic, sensuous surroundings who fall into each other's arms and beds already in a state of high arousal and proceed to have thrilling intercourse and earth-shaking orgasms.

The real sex of real people is not like this. Real sex is good sex, not perfect sex. Real sex is not a performance, and it is not the same every time. Sex is about the two of you, enjoying one another, giving yourselves to one another, receiving from one another. Real sex includes touch that ranges from the affectionate to the sensual to the erotic. It includes intercourse but can accept with equanimity sexual encounters that for one reason or another don't go there.

The more flexible and relational a sexual partnership you can cultivate in your marriage, the greater will be the intimacy you can enjoy with your partner right now, in the early years of your marriage. And that flexible and relational sexual partnership will serve you well as your marriage matures. Instead of defining sex as a pass-fail test that you are bound sooner or later to fail, you will have developed a range of options for relating sexually to your partner that will allow you to continue to enjoy sexual intimacy throughout your lifetimes, whatever changes may be brought about in your lives and bodies due to aging or to illness or disability.

Christian faith ought to be an encouragement in this regard. Christian faith is about living in the real world, not a Hollywood or Madison Avenue–inspired fantasy world. And Christian marriage is marriage for the long haul, marriage not just for youth but for midlife and beyond. Sexuality and sensuality are part of marriage. They can and ought to be valuable elements of marital intimacy, throughout the seasons of a couple's life.

Fidelity

With all the emphasis placed by many Christians on the importance of how people conduct themselves sexually before marriage, it could seem that appropriate sexual behavior after marriage just takes care of itself. In particular, it could seem that fidelity in marriage is automatic. The thought seems to be that once a person has a licit sexual partner, he or she will stick to that partner and not be shopping around for anyone else.

We all know it doesn't necessarily work that way. Most husbands and wives are faithful to one another. But a significant minority (researchers have estimated the numbers at 20-25 percent of men and 10-15 percent of women) are not.[8] And the truth is that we live in a culture that encourages infidelity. Novelty and variety are portrayed as essential elements in the good life, and nowhere more so than where sex is concerned. If this is true, how could anyone possibly expect to be sexually satisfied over a lifetime with the same partner?

Christians are as susceptible to these pressures as anybody else. "I am afraid of the monotony of marriage," confessed one person. "I wonder if even Christian married couples sometimes find themselves wondering how sex would be with someone other than their spouse." "I am scared of boredom within my marriage," wrote another. "I am afraid my sex life will die down and I will consider sex a chore, instead of something incredibly wonderful and beautiful."

There are both practical and theological responses to this cultural emphasis on novelty and excitement. Practically speaking, unfettered access to a continuous stream of novel sexual experiences does not, in fact, lead to satisfaction. There is a reason, in other words, for the constant proliferation of pornographic material and sexual solicitations on the web and elsewhere: novelty for novelty's sake just leaves people wanting more.

As counterintuitive as it may seem (at least to those caught up in the restless quest for more and better), sexual satisfaction is not about novelty. It is about connection, relationship and openness to intimacy. True eroticism is not incompatible with familiarity. True eroticism is grounded in the kind of mutual surrender that can be enacted only by partners who have learned or are in the process of learning to trust each other with their lives and with their bodies.

---

[8]Barry W. McCarthy and Michael E. Metz, *Men's Sexual Health* (New York: Routledge, 2008), p. 167.

Another practical reality is that while infidelity might introduce a certain kind of sexual excitement into your life, it will also introduce other kinds of excitement that are much less pleasant—namely, the upheaval and pain that come with a seriously injured or permanently broken marriage. Affairs are extraordinarily damaging to marriages, spouses, children and the broader communities of which individuals and families are a part. Whether or not an affair results in divorce, it will certainly hurt you and everyone with whom you are in relationship.

Rather than hope or assume an affair will never happen to you, it is better actively to prevent one. Talk with your partner about what kinds of situations might make either of you vulnerable to an affair. Agree that if a situation like that comes up, you will talk with one another about it rather than impulsively acting on opportunity. If either of you ever actually is unfaithful, talk with your partner about the event within twenty-four hours of its occurrence. A cover-up can be more damaging than the affair itself.[9]

Christians, of course, commit themselves to fidelity in marriage not just for practical reasons but for theological ones. Christian marriage reflects the relationship of God with God's people. God is faithful to those whom he calls into relationship with himself, and for whom he gives himself in love. Christian spouses are called to do the same. This is not natural; it is a gift and a calling. Fidelity in marriage offers an opportunity to live a life that is shaped by the gospel and open to the transformation inherent in the gospel.

---

[9]For these guidelines, see ibid., pp. 167-68.

7

Hospitality

Welcoming Children and Other Strangers

MANY MODERN AMERICANS ARE INCLINED to think of marriage as something that exists primarily for their own benefit and for that of their spouse. We get married because we want to be together. More specifically, we want to be alone together. We want to enjoy one another's company without the intrusion or involvement of others. Public life, with its market-driven exchanges of goods and services for money, necessarily involves interactions with people we do not know or care to know. Private life is seen as valuable precisely to the degree that it forms a refuge from such intrusions. A husband and wife should be able to shut the door behind them, we think, and have their relationship and their marriage to themselves.

This privatized, inwardly focused vision of marriage is not entirely congruent with the portrait of Christian marriage that we find in Scripture. Scripture presents marriage as a form or image of Christian community. Marriage is akin to the relationship between Christ and the church, Paul tells us (Ephesians 5:32), and that relationship, while deeply intimate, is not purely private. Rather, it is founded upon and characterized by hospitality, by the welcoming of the stranger and the consequent and sometimes surprising transformation of both the stranger and the welcoming community.

Hospitality goes back to the beginning of the history of God with both the human race and the people of Israel. When God created our first parents, he placed them in a garden he had made to be their home, and gave them food to eat and work to do. When Adam and Eve were expelled from the garden of Eden, even then God's parting gesture was to clothe them (Genesis 3:21). And when the people of Israel entered the land of promise, Moses taught them to remember that they had been wandering strangers, and God had welcomed them, feeding and clothing and sheltering them and bringing them home. In response, it was their duty to care for the aliens and strangers in their midst (Deuteronomy 26:1-15).

In the New Testament we see the boundaries of the people of God expanded to include Gentiles (that is, non-Jews). The Gentiles had been strangers to the covenants of promise, Paul reminded them, but in Christ they had been united to the Old Testament people of God. "So then you are no longer strangers and sojourners, but you are fellow citizens with the saints and members of the household of God" (Ephesians 2:19). And as before, God's welcome was to be reenacted in the lives of his people. "Practice hospitality," wrote Paul to the church at Rome (Romans 12:13). "Practice hospitality," echoed the apostle Peter, writing to the church at large (1 Peter 4:9).

Hospitality does not do away with privacy or intimacy. On the contrary: hospitality requires boundaries. You cannot invite anybody in if there is no distinction between "in" and "out." But at the same time, you cannot invite anybody in if your walls have no doors, or if you keep such doors shut tight all the time. This is as true of Christian marriage as it is of other forms of Christian community. Christian marriage has deeply private elements. Among these is the sexual relationship between husband and wife. And at the very same time the life-giving nature of sexual relations means that here, in the exclusivity and the privacy of the marriage bed, is one of the primary opportunities for hospitality that is given to any Christian couple: the opportunity to welcome children.

Of course sexual relations are about more than children. And the bearing and rearing of children are not the only ways that Christian husbands and wives can—or should—respond to the invitation to practice hospitality. But the openness and vulnerability and potential for transformation that are intrinsic to hospitality make this a helpful category to keep in mind as we think about what it means to open our lives and marriages to children and other strangers.

Why Christians Have Children

There is a sense in which it is obvious why anyone has children. People have sex, and where there is sex, there are children. Yes, there are sexual acts that are by their very nature nonprocreative, and not every potentially procreative sexual act results in a child. But in the ordinary run of things, the members of the human race engage in a lot of potentially procreative sex, and a lot of children are born as a result.

People also have children because they want them. They like children. They may remember their own childhoods happily, and look forward to enjoying the childhoods of their own sons or daughters. They may appreciate the roles their parents have played in their lives, and look forward to handing on those gifts to their own children. They want to have children who are biologically "theirs," who will carry on their family lines, who will give them grandchildren, who will survive them when they die.

On the other hand, there is such a thing as contraception, and in the modern world there can be strong incentives to use it. In preindustrial societies, children were economic assets to their parents. More children meant more hands to work on the farm. But in most modern societies, children are economic liabilities. Children have to be tended and clothed and schooled at significant cost to their parents for eighteen years or more, at which point it is not unheard of for them to move far away and not be available to care for their parents in their old age. You might stand a better chance of being taken care of in your old age if you didn't have children, saved your money, and hired caregivers at the end of life.

It can also be difficult to combine rearing children with pursuing other opportunities in life. Societies that require women to choose between career and children typically see birth rates plummet as women follow the money.[1] And even in countries with more family-friendly social policies, or in which parents are supposedly free to choose to combine family and career, very often the reality is that if you wish to rise to the top of your profession, you do better to have few or no children.[2] And how many more people does the world really need? Are children good for the planet? Or is it a selfish overuse of the world's resources to have children, or to have more than one or two?

In a Christian understanding, children are not just a fact of life, and not just something to have or not to have, depending on how you weigh the pros and cons. Children are the fruit of marriage. The creation of humans as male and female, and the joining of a man and a woman in marriage, have among their specific purposes the bearing and rearing of children. "Be fruitful and multiply" are God's words, not just to human beings in general, but to

[1]See, for example, Katrin Bennhold, "In Germany, a Tradition Falls, and Women Rise," *New York Times,* January 17, 2010.
[2]David Leonhardt, "A Market Punishing to Mothers," *New York Times,* August 3, 2010.

husbands and wives in particular, of whose one flesh children are born (Genesis 1:28; 2:24).

Children are a blessing. This is, to be truthful, not always obvious. Our world is both a finite and a fallen place, and its limitations and corruptions appear as plainly in relation to childbearing and child rearing as anywhere. Longed-for pregnancies may end in miscarriage. Childbirth is painful and potentially life-threatening for both mother and child. Children die young, leaving their parents bereft. Children turn out badly, breaking their parents' hearts. They kill each other, like Cain and Abel (Genesis 4:8); or cheat each other, like Jacob and Esau (Genesis 27); or betray each other, like Joseph and his brothers (Genesis 37).

And yet Christian Scripture portrays children as both a blessing and a promise. God's promise to Abraham is one of descendants as numerous as the stars in the sky (Genesis 15:5). "Blessed is every one who fears the LORD," says the psalmist. "Your wife will be like a fruitful vine within your house; your children will be like olive shoots around your table" (Psalm 128:1, 3-4). In the day to come, Isaiah says, even the barren will be fruitful (Isaiah 54:1). In that day God's people "shall not labor in vain, or bear children for calamity; for they shall be the offspring of the blessed of the LORD, and their children with them" (Isaiah 65:23).

The Gospels relativize the status of parenthood and childbearing. To a woman who cries out to Jesus, "Blessed is the womb that bore you, and the breasts that you sucked," Jesus replies, "Blessed rather are those who hear the word of God and keep it" (Luke 11:27-28). But at the same time, children are everywhere included in Jesus' ministry. Jesus heals sick children (Matthew 17:14-18); he restores dead children to life (Luke 7:11-17); he feeds children (Mark 5:21-43); he feeds other people with food shared by children (John 6:1-14). "Let the children come to me," Jesus says, "and do not hinder them; for to such belongs the kingdom of heaven" (Matthew 19:14).

In the life of the church we find all of these themes continued. Children are a relative rather than an absolute good. Christians are under no obligation to marry or to bear or beget children. God does not depend on Christians to have children in order to supply the next generation of believers. It is not up to us to have children in order to keep the church going. On the contrary, God adds believers to the church through witness and conversion, regardless of the identity or faith of their parents.

At the same time, children are integral to the life and hope of the Christian community. As the apostle Peter says, the promises of the gospel are "to you and to your children" (Acts 2:39). The care and education of other people's children have long been among the works to which Christians, especially members of vowed religious orders, have devoted themselves. And when Christians marry, children are among the purposes and the hoped-for blessings of marriage. Prayers for children are thus a part of traditional marriage liturgies, as, for example, that of the Book of Common Prayer: "Bestow on [this couple], if it is your will, the gift and heritage of children, and the grace to bring them up to know you, to love you, and to serve you."

In light of the positive place accorded children in Christian Scripture and tradition, and the simple facts that marriage involves sex, and sex tends to lead to children, it is interesting to note the considerable skittishness with which many Christian young people view the prospect of childbearing and child rearing. This is true even—or especially—among those who are newly married or on the brink of marriage. For the vast majority of those who say they want children, their preferred timing is "not yet."

Why not now? They're not ready. They are not financially secure. They are not settled in their careers. They are busy. They

enjoy the freedom of being able to come and go without considering the needs or schedules of children. They have, in many cases,
been explicitly taught that marital satisfaction decreases after the
arrival of children, or that having a baby "too soon" is bad for your
marriage. So, they decide to wait. How long? Five years. By the
time this comfortably longish interval has passed, they suppose,
they will be "ready."

There are also a considerable number of young people who
express uneasiness, not just about the practical implications of
parenthood, but about the whole notion of bearing or begetting
children. Very often these young people do hope to rear children
(although also "not yet"), but their plan is to adopt them rather
than give birth to them. "When my wife and I talked about our
reasons for getting married, procreation was not one of them,"
wrote one young man. "We believe that adoption is a model that
more closely resembles Christ's redefinition of family."

He is not alone. Isn't it selfish, young people ask, to bring a
child into the world when there are so many children already born
who need homes and families? The world is a scary place; there
are enough hurting people in it already. "So many children are
already in misery and are already suffering. Why bring more tears
into the world when you could bring a few smiles?" wrote one
young woman. "I cannot allow myself to bring a child of my own
into the world if I can support the life of one that no one wants,"
wrote another.

We suspect that part of what lies behind this stated preference
for adoption is a romanticized ignorance of the practical realities
of childbearing and adoption. Most Americans view adoption fa-
vorably, but very few take any concrete steps toward adopting, and
even fewer actually adopt. One contributing factor is the high cost
of many adoptions (often reaching into the tens of thousands of
dollars). Another is the fact that the numbers of children available

for adoption are relatively low, and of those who are available, many are children whose particular needs make them difficult to place. In the year 2001 there were just over four million babies born in the United States. In the same year there were about 127,000 adoptions, 40 percent of which were adoptions by a stepparent or other relative. The adoption of children whom "no one wants," in other words, is quite rare, amounting in any given year to little more than 1 percent of the number of children added to families through birth.[3]

More seriously, the way that too many young people talk about adoption reflects a serious misunderstanding of the nature of adoption. If you adopt a child, the feeling seems to be, you are not responsible for his or her existence. You are not adding to the world's problems, but are only trying to ameliorate them by parenting other people's abandoned children. It's a win-win situation: you get to be a parent, but nobody can blame you for having the kid in the first place.

This is not what adoption is about. Adoption is not a sort of free pass into the world of parenthood. Adoption is a way of providing for the nurturance of a child in a secure and loving environment when the child's own parents cannot do this themselves. Adoption can have the happy effect of bringing a child into the home of parents who long for one (or more), but it is about the child first and only secondarily about the adopting parents. And there is in-

---

[3]There were 4,025,933 births in the U.S. in 2001 (Joyce A. Martin et al., "Births: Final Data for 2001," *National Vital Statistics Reports* 51, no. 2 [December 18, 2002]: 3). In the same year there were 127,407 adoptions, approximately 19,000 of which were international adoptions ("How Many Children Were Adopted in 2000 and 2001? Numbers and Trends," Child Welfare Information Gateway <www.childwelfare.gov/pubs/s_adopted/s_adopteda.cfm>). About half of all domestic adoptions are by someone related to the child, including stepparents ("Adopted Children and Stepchildren: 2000," Census 2000 Special Reports, Issued October 2003). Subtracting 19,000 international adoptions from 127,407 total adoptions yields 108,407 domestic adoptions. Half of these were adoptions by relatives; the remaining half (adoptions by nonrelatives) equals 54,204, which is 1.3 percent of 4,025,933.

evitably both loss and gain for all of the parties involved in adoption: the relinquishing parents, the adopting parents and the child. It is possible for the gains far to outweigh the losses for all concerned; but adoption is always a complex response to a complex situation, and never just a simple way to do an end run around whatever qualms one might feel about childbearing.

Contraception

Most fundamentally, we believe, the attitude of many young people toward both childbearing and adoption reflects the profound way in which the ready availability of reliable contraception alters the moral calculus of childbearing. It used to be that a decision to marry was tantamount to the decision to become a parent (except in cases when the woman was known to be past the age of childbearing). Married couples did not have to "decide" to have children; in the vast majority of cases, children just came.

Contraception changes that. Where contraception is the order of the day, children do not just come, or at least the sense is that they should not. Children are now seen not as fruit, but as choices. Individuals and couples can choose when to have children and whether to have children, and in fact they must so choose—a decision not to contracept is just as much a decision as is the decision to contracept.

Once children are choices, the whole nature of the game changes. The option of controlling one's fertility becomes the duty to control one's fertility. It is wrong, or so our contraceptive culture teaches us, to have children under any but ideal circumstances. To have a child too soon is wrong. To have too many children is wrong. To have a child who might impose a burden on anybody else (by, for example, being handicapped) is wrong. To have any child whose existence has not been adequately planned for is wrong. Is it any wonder that many young people find themselves thinking that maybe they don't want children at all, or maybe they would rather adopt other people's children, or at the very least maybe they had better wait and have children later, when they feel up to it?

When children are choices, the most fundamental question concerning any child or potential child is, "Do you want it?" Pregnancies are viewed as good or bad depending upon whether they were "planned." Since nearly half of all pregnancies among American women are not planned, this is a lot of problematic pregnancies. Forty percent of those pregnancies are deliberately terminated, as the abortion industry steps in to provide backup for those who did not contracept or whose contraception failed.[4]

When children are choices, it also comes quickly to seem that anyone who wants a child should be able to have one. The flip side of contraception thus is reproductive technology. Contraception promises (not always truthfully) that pregnancy can be prevented at will; reproductive technology promises (also not always truthfully) that pregnancy can be created at will. The appeal of reproductive medicine is of course clear: infertility is one of the oldest sorrows known to humans, and the birth of a child to a couple who had thought themselves unable to have one is as close to a miracle as any of us might ever hope to see.

Modern reproductive technology, however, is more of a Pandora's box than many of us would like to admit. People who would never dream of having an affair find themselves thinking it would

---

[4]Those who did not contracept are more likely to be poor; those whose contraception failed are more likely to be wealthy. More abortions are performed on poor women than on wealthy women, as the poor outnumber the wealthy, and poor women tend to have more unplanned pregnancies. But wealthy women terminate a greater proportion of their unplanned pregnancies than do poor women. After all, they have a plan, and this child isn't part of it. As one researcher notes, "Highly educated people are less likely to have unintended pregnancies, but they are also less tolerant of them." Stanley K. Henshaw, of the Guttmacher Institute, quoted in Peter Brimelow, "Who Has Abortions?" *Forbes*, October 18, 1999.

be a good idea to bring a third party into their marriage bed in the form of a sperm donor or an ovum donor. People who would never dream of having an abortion find themselves creating whole freezers full of embryos as spares in case this cycle of in vitro fertilization fails to produce a pregnancy.

People who firmly believe that marriage is God's intended context for the bearing and rearing of children find themselves shocked when single women and same-sex couples turn to sperm banks and surrogates in pursuit of the children they want, never realizing that these men and women are only following the example set for them by the heterosexual couples who are the fertility clinics' primary customers. Gay or straight, single or married, they all want children, and they are determined to have them, no matter whose body parts they have to use in the process.

It is an ancient conviction of the church that marriage, sex and children go together and should not deliberately be separated. For this reason, the Roman Catholic Church teaches that every marital act must be open to conception (that is, that contraception is always wrong) and that conception must never be removed from the marital bed (that is, that reproductive technology is always wrong). But you do not have to be a Roman Catholic or to agree with either of these propositions to see that many of the assumptions embedded in both contraception and reproductive technology are deeply problematic from a Christian theological perspective, and easily lead to deeply problematic behavior on the part of Christians. Can we really receive children as gifts when contraception teaches us jealously to guard our fertility? Can we really bear children as fruit when reproductive technology teaches us to view children as manufacturing projects?

If there are good reasons to contracept (and we think that there can be), there are equally compelling reasons to contracept mindfully rather than mindlessly. Contraception is not just another personal hygiene product, like toothpaste or deodorant. Contraception affects your body, it affects your sexual relationship with your spouse, it affects your marriage as a whole, it affects your entire way of being in the world. It is something to think about, and something to talk about.

Among the first things to think about is whether contraception really delivers what it promises—namely, freedom, not merely from babies but also from worry about babies. "I stopped by the pharmacy the other day to get some more of my birth control pills," wrote one young wife. "I have a ten-dollar copay a month. As I was standing in line it hit me: I pay thirty-three cents a day not to get pregnant. It's like a variation of the old saying: 'Thirty-three cents a day keeps the babies away.'" So far, the thirty-three cents a day had kept the babies away. It had not kept worry away. "Probably what has been on my mind the most since I got married is the fear of getting pregnant. I don't mean the thought of getting pregnant. I mean the deep, gut-level *fear* of getting pregnant."

Can we really delight in sex if we are consumed with fear at the possible consequences of it, despite our best efforts to wall ourselves off from those consequences? Contracepted sex starts to look like a range of other denatured products now available to the modern consumer: decaffeinated coffee, diet soda, fat-free ice cream—all of which are supposed to enable limitless consumption of these commodities while preventing any untoward consequences, and none of which anyone really enjoys.[5]

Why then are you using contraception, or considering its use? The culture of contraception stands ready to encourage you to fear what a baby would do to your life, your plans, your marriage, your body. Contraception also fosters illusions of control: you can and should be able to have the child you want, when you want it, and

---

[5]See the discussion of this in R. J. Snell, "The Gift of Good Sex: Thinking Contraception Anew," *Covenant Quarterly* (2008): 31.

not when you don't. As Christians, can we resist these temptations, using contraception prudentially while not succumbing to fear or to the illusion that our lives are our own to control as we see fit?

How will you choose one contraceptive method over another?[6] The birth-control industry is moving more and more toward contraceptive methods that are long-lasting and entirely separate from either sex or relationship. On its invention fifty years ago, the birth-control pill was hailed as a great advance over barrier methods, precisely because a woman did not have to negotiate its use with a sexual partner. Now the sense is that a once-a-day pill is too much trouble; people need "fool-proof contraceptives that require almost no thought or action."[7]

The obvious problem with this is that where contraception is foolproof and thoughtless, sex will be too. Is that really what any of us wants? Is that really compatible with Christian notions of what sex and marriage and human life itself are really all about? It might be that you will choose a contraceptive method that requires thought, perhaps on the part of both spouses, precisely because you want your sexual relationship to reflect thoughtfulness and cooperation.

A final question to consider when thinking about the use of contraception has to do with pregnancy. What would you do if, despite your contraceptive use, you were to conceive? Many con-

---

[6]Contraceptive methods exist on a continuum, with some requiring more attention and involvement from one or both partners and others requiring less. Natural family planning requires abstention from sexual relations for about ten days a month, during the most fertile period of a woman's cycle. Barrier methods have to be used each time a couple has sexual relations. Oral contraceptives have to be taken daily but are independent of sexual relations. Hormonal patches and implants can last for months or years. For information about the use and effectiveness of all these approaches to the prevention and regulation of pregnancy, see Anthony L. Komaroff, ed., *Harvard Medical School Family Health Guide* (New York: Free Press, 2005), pp. 68-76.

[7]Shari Roan, "'The pill': 50 years after," *Los Angeles Times*, May 4, 2010, citing James Trussell, director of Princeton University's Office of Population Research.

traceptive methods are very effective, but few are guaranteed 100 percent. The fact is, people become pregnant all the time, and not always when they are planning on it. Openness to possibility is part of Christian faithfulness. Openness to children is part of Christian marriage. Can we use contraception in ways that are compatible with an openness to children?

A theological alternative to considering pregnancy and child-bearing as things we must control and fend off under all but ideal circumstances might be to view the bearing and rearing of children through the lenses of faith, hope and love. By faith Christians trust that God's care extends to them even in the midst of so unpredictable and risk-laden an enterprise as having children. The world is full of dangers from which we cannot fully protect our children. We cannot know ahead of time precisely what challenges will confront us as parents, or how we will rise to meet them. But by faith we trust that God's love and guidance and protection will accompany us even into this unknown territory, and that we will find peace and blessing there.

In hope Christians look forward to the gift of children, recognizing that this gift may or may not be given exactly when or as they expect. To hope for children does not exclude planning for them. But human plans for just about anything are notorious for being disrupted by a reality that turns out some other way. Framing the desire for children in terms of hope—a hope for children now or children later, a hope for more children or for fewer children, a hope for healthy children rather than children who are ill or impaired in some way—can be part of helping us to receive with thanksgiving and humility our children as they actually come to us.

And it is with a love akin to God's own creative love that Christian husbands and wives give themselves to one another in sexual relations that are open to children. The notion that having children is "selfish" is something we learn from a self-absorbed and self-protective culture, not from Christian tradition. In a Christian understanding, an openness to children is the very opposite of selfishness. Whereas contraception requires the withholding of one's fertility from the spouse, noncontracepted sexual relations allow for the complete self-giving of each spouse to the other, and make possible the blossoming of that gift of self in the creation of a new life.

Not every marriage that is open to children will receive them. Sometimes conjugal love bears fruit in other ways. And Christ does indeed redefine family in such a way that all Christians, married or not, are called to a hospitality that reaches beyond the lines of blood and kin. For some this may mean adoption or foster parenting. For others it may mean welcoming or ministering to adults or children in other ways. But marital love is meant to be creative, and an openness to children—perhaps not in every conjugal act, but certainly over the course of a marriage as a whole—is one central way in which that creativity has opportunity to take root, to flower and to bear fruit.

What Children Need

Every family is different. Every child is different. The nap times or feeding schedules that work for your first child may be very different from the ones that work for the second or third; the decisions about school or sports or pocket money that suit one family may be very different from those that suit another family. While it can be fine to think about what one's preferences might be with respect to some of these things, a lot of the specific decisions will have to be made later, after the children have arrived and you have begun to get to know them and to get a sense of what they and you together need and want.

On the other hand, there are some things about children and

child rearing that do merit serious consideration ahead of time. Chief among these is the simple fact that if you get married, you may well have children, and it is possible that they may arrive at any time. Precisely because most young couples today assume that they either will wait or ought to wait to have children, the temptation is strong to wait also for any detailed consideration of what the arrival of children might mean for their relationship. After all, five years (or whatever the time horizon is) seems like a long time off. Why think now about something so far in the future?

It is better to talk about it. If you are not yet married, talking with a potential partner about what you would do if you conceived a child "ahead of schedule" can help you discern whether it is wise for you to marry each other. What happens when you talk about this? Are you able to agree that, although it might be hard, you would be able to find a way to make room for this child and to embark together on the journey of parenthood? Or does the subject of pregnancy seem to lead inevitably to arguments or to uncomfortable silence or to a feeling of impending doom? After a conversation about unplanned pregnancy, do you feel more confident in the health and strength of your relationship, or less so?

Talking ahead of time about the possibility of pregnancy can also help a couple to respond positively and as a team to news of actual pregnancy, whether that happens on schedule or not. The oft-reported changes in marital satisfaction after the arrival of children turn out to be strongly related to whether children are welcomed equally by both of their parents. When parents disagree about whether or when to conceive, or one or both of them are ambivalent about whether they want to be parents at all, marital satisfaction tends to decrease after the birth of a child. But when both parents are involved in planning a pregnancy, or they are united in welcoming a pregnancy that was not planned, marital satisfaction tends to remain the same or to increase after the child is born.[8]

The primary reason for working together to welcome a child, of course, is not that it is good for you, but that it is good for the child. Children are unable to provide for themselves. Not unlike travelers in the ancient world, who often depended on the kindness of strangers for meals and shelter, children are born into the world naked and hungry and dependent for their very lives upon being taken in and fed and clothed and otherwise nurtured by people they have never met before, namely, their parents. They depend, in other words, on hospitality.

Hospitality does not require perfection on the part of those who offer it nor those who receive it. It can be tempting to believe that it does. The perfect host or hostess, we imagine, is one whose house is immaculate, whose table is beautiful, whose food is elegant, and whose parties always come off without a hitch. The perfect guest, in turn, is well dressed and well behaved, a charming and witty conversationalist who always pleases and never annoys and goes home promptly at the end of the evening.

And so we are sometimes inclined to believe concerning parents and children. A good parent, we suppose, is a perfect parent. Good parents know all of the answers and never make any mistakes. They are endlessly patient, endlessly nurturing, endlessly loving. And good children are perfect too. They are beautiful and healthy and intelligent and obedient. They never demand more from their parents than the parents are prepared to give, and they always reflect well on the families of which they are a part.

Of course these are fantasies. We all know that real life is not like this. But powerful currents at work in our society encourage us to believe that it ought to be. Parents—and especially moth-

---

[8]Stephanie Coontz, "Till Children Do Us Part," *New York Times*, February 5, 2009.

ers—are encouraged to think that their job is to optimize their children's experiences in every respect.[9] Prenatal testing and abortion are used to fend off the birth of children who are deemed defective.[10] And reproductive technology is increasingly marketed as a means of selecting children with desirable traits: the right sex, the right color of eyes and hair, the right amount of intelligence or height or athletic ability.[11]

Granted, the money to pay for what we imagine will be perfect children, along with the resources to obsess over trying to be the perfect parent, are much more available to the wealthy than they are to the general population. But the temptation is there for all of us to suppose that parenthood is about perfection. "I feel so inadequate to be a mother," wrote one engaged woman. "I do not know if I will be ready even after waiting five years. If I have a child earlier than that I will be a wreck! It is a relief to think that hospitality means doing the best I can to welcome a new baby, and not having to be perfect."

Even without any pressure to be perfect, most of us would like to be able to do the best job by our children that we can. We have all been shaped by our own childhoods, and bear in our own selves the marks of our upbringings. Where we were well-served by our parents, we tend to want to do similarly well for our own children, so that they can prosper as we did. And where our parents fell short, we tend to want to do a better job than our parents did, so that our children will not have to suffer as we did.

Having had good parents, or parents who did well in particular ways, is no guarantee that you will be a good parent yourself. But

---

[9]See, for example, Judith Warner, *Perfect Madness: Motherhood in the Age of Anxiety* (New York: Riverhead, 2005).

[10]Amy Harmon, "Prenatal Test Puts Down Syndrome in Hard Focus," *New York Times*, May 9, 2007.

[11]Gautam Naik, "A Baby, Please. Blond, Freckles—Hold the Colic," *Wall Street Journal*, February 12, 2009.

we do learn a lot of what we know about parenting from our own parents, and it is easier to follow a good example than it is to reject a bad example. On the other hand, having had bad parents, or parents who failed in significant ways, does not doom you. It just means you have to be particularly intentional about reflecting on the example you have been set, and particularly creative in thinking about what might be some better alternatives.

It is never too early to begin to set in place good foundations for parenting. The needs of children—for security, nurturance, intimacy, love—are essentially the same as those of older human beings, only more so. So even if you never have children, it will not hurt you or your partner to work toward being the sort of people who could be good parents. In particular, it is never too early to put away the kinds of bad habits that make it difficult to be even an adequate parent. No yelling, no hitting, and no drinking to excess are good places to start. Violence and alcohol abuse often take the form of generational curses, because it is so common for these patterns to be handed down from parents to children. But it is possible to break the cycle. One young man wrote,

> My uncle says he used to fear nothing more than becoming either his father or his stepfather. He never wanted his children to experience a home like the one he grew up in, so he did everything he could to prevent it. He stopped drinking. He never yells. He believes that if there is a problem, his girls and he can talk through it. Whatever he is doing, it works. His children are two of the most well-mannered, adorable little girls I have ever had the pleasure of knowing. My uncle's love for them has a maturity you don't always see in other families.

Children also need their parents to be fully supportive and inclusive of one another as parents. Children need substantive relationships with both of their parents, and this is far more likely to happen when mothers and fathers respect and appreciate each other as parents. Part of growing into your roles as a mother and as a father, therefore, is recognizing and appreciating your mate's strengths and making room in your family for both of you to participate actively in rearing your children.

This is not something that happens automatically. Mothers and fathers have different relationships with their children, most obviously in the fact that it is mothers who give birth to children and who can choose in most instances to nurse them as infants. This deeply intimate physical bond between mothers and children can be intimidating to fathers. It is not always obvious, either to them or to their wives, what their place is in this newly expanded family. Sometimes fathers respond by stepping back and leaving the parenting to mom.

Mothers sometimes encourage this. Sometimes women plan for this even before they are mothers. Every so often we hear someone offer the opinion that in that far-off day when she becomes a mother, she will expect to have more say in child-rearing decisions than does her spouse, since after all, she gave birth to the child. Besides, she will add, she was better brought up than was her intended spouse, and so she expects to be a better parent than he will be.

To which we can only say, don't do this! Husbands and fathers should not be made outsiders in their own homes and relegated to the role of second-class parent. Mothers should not install themselves in splendid isolation upon the parenting throne, or be encouraged by anyone else to assume such a status. Child rearing is a big job, plenty big enough for both parents to share in its challenges and in its pleasures. Your children need you both, and they will be much happier if you both cooperate as mutually respectful equals in parenting them.

You are likely to be happier too. Our individualistic and specialized society tells us that the more important something is, the more important it is either to keep it all to yourself or to hand it over to the experts. Where child rearing is concerned, it is more often mothers who think they want to do it all themselves, and more often fathers who are inclined to let the experts (namely mothers) take care of it. In truth, though, the more important something is, the more important it is to share it. Shared undertakings are the most exhilarating; shared accomplishments are the most rewarding. Child rearing is the central project of many marriages. Let it be a shared one.

Hospitality to a child does not end with the child's birth. It continues anew through every stage of that child's life and growth. Just as you get used to your baby and feel like you know what you are doing, your infant grows into a toddler and you have to start all over again. Then just when you feel you have a handle on the terrible twos, your child turns three and now you have a pre-schooler and have to figure that out. Then you have a kindergartener, and then a gradeschooler, and then a tween.

And then one day your child enters puberty, and it is as if in the night someone stole away your sweet puppy and replaced him or her with a moody cat that doesn't want to be petted or played with or acknowledged in any way—and you have to figure out anew what it means to welcome this stranger. And then the aloof feline stage is itself succeeded by the pleasures and challenges that come with seeing your son or daughter grow into maturity and become no longer simply a child, but an adult child.

At every point in the process parents and children have the opportunity to come together in the complex encounter that is hospitality. Hospitality is not a one-way street, with hosts endlessly offering out of their abundance and guests endlessly taking in their neediness. Hospitality is a dimension of the kingdom of God, in which the last shall be first and the first shall be last, and in which hosts can all of a sudden realize they are guests at their own table, at the head of which sits Christ himself: "Truly, I say to you, as you did it to one of the least of these my brethren, you did it to me" (Matthew 25:40).

Hospitality to children comes with a cost. Emotionally, physically and financially, rearing children is a lot of work. But it is work that in the experience of many parents is rewarded more amply than they could have imagined. Children do not dilute or detract from Christian lives or Christian marriages; they add to and enrich them. We begin with no idea what our children will be like, or what we will be like as parents. We become people who cannot imagine what our lives would be like without the individuals who have entered our families as our children.

Beyond Child Rearing

Hospitality neither begins nor ends with the welcoming of children. There are opportunities throughout all of our lives to welcome others and to be welcomed by them. Some of these opportunities may have to do not with strangers but with people who are already members of our families or circles of friends. We live in a culture in which it is assumed that an individual married couple will establish their own household and will share it only with their own children, if and when they have any. But extended-family or communal living arrangements have been common in many times and places, and can be beneficial and enriching for all concerned.

A younger couple may accept an offer to live with one or another set of parents. A couple in midlife may extend an offer to an elderly parent or parents to share their home. Family members or friends of any age or marital status may choose to combine their households for economic reasons, or to facilitate shared child-rearing arrangements, or simply because they prefer to share their lives more intimately than they could if they lived separately. Such combined households run counter to cultural ideals of independence and isolation, but are entirely in keeping with the communal nature of the kingdom of God.

We also live in a very mobile culture, in which there are, at any time, many people who are far from home or whose family members live at a distance. The practice of hospitality offers a way to draw into our family circles people who are new to our communities, who are only temporarily residing there, or who live alone with no family nearby. If you have a large home and a small family, perhaps an extra bedroom can become home to a person from another country or someone else in need of housing or care. If your house is already bursting at the seams, perhaps hospitality can take the form of an invitation to dinner, or a meal carried to the home of someone who is sick or alone.

When there are children in the home, hospitality toward their friends becomes an important dimension of Christian family life. All children need adults in their lives in addition to their parents, and many children come from family situations that render them particularly in need of hospitality from sources outside their families. Children from abusive or neglectful homes may actually need another place to live; children from less seriously troubled homes need a glad and generous welcome from adults who can show them by word and by example that there is reason to hope for better things. People in a wide variety of life situations can play significant parts in the lives of children other than their own, but parents of children of similar ages may be particularly well-positioned to see such needs and meet them.

In all these ways and more, Christians are called to respond to the welcome that they have received from God himself by extending that welcome further into the world. Marriage brings with it the invitation to practice hospitality in ways suited to the married state. The intimate and exclusive bond that exists between individual husbands and wives is designed to bear fruit in the form of a home and a life that are open to relationship with those children or others whom Christ leads to our doors. As we welcome these strangers, we may come face to face with Christ himself.

8

Households

LOVE DOES NOT PAY THE BILLS. It doesn't do the laundry or clean the bathroom, either. But all these things—and more—have to get done, or even the most easygoing, nonmaterialistic couple are going to find themselves unable to support and nurture one another and their children, and to contribute to the larger communities of which they are a part. Marriage is about love, yes. But marriage is also about production and consumption and finances. Marriage is about economics.

The word *economics* is related to the Greek word *oikonomia,* meaning "household management." Supporting and sustaining a household in a market economy requires money, which has to come from somewhere. Another thing required to support and sustain a household is the time and labor involved in making a home: buying the groceries (or cultivating a garden), cooking the meals, washing the clothes, cleaning the house. That also has to come from somewhere. And if there are children in the home, childcare enters the equation—someone has to do that too.

Our culture encourages us to view only some of these activities as genuinely productive—namely, the ones for which we are paid.

Paid work is calculated (and taxed) as part of the gross domestic product. Unpaid housework and childcare are not. Retirement benefits go disproportionately to people who earn paychecks. So does health insurance. Employers are inclined to view continuous full-time presence in the paid workforce as a precondition for hiring and promotion. A person who "takes time off" for child rearing (for example) is likely to be seen as unserious and unproductive. The assumption is that if you are not earning money, you are "not working."

Christian Scripture and tradition take a different view. God's own work is represented in Scripture as having to do, more often than not, with the provision of food and clothing and shelter. God creates a home for his people in Eden, in the promised land, in the new Jerusalem. He feeds them with manna, with loaves and fishes, with the Eucharist. He clothed our first parents with skins as they went out into the wilderness; he clothed the Israelites during their wanderings; he clothes us with righteousness when we enter into the kingdom.

If all these things are work when God does them, then they are work when men and women do them too. The direct provision of food and clothing and shelter is just as productive, and just as much a contribution to the economy of a household or a larger community, as is work that earns a paycheck. A family needs money if it is to survive, but its members need nurturance and care too. Husbands and wives have the opportunity to form a partnership in which together they provide one another and their children with these various necessities. Making a living and making a home—and managing the money that comes in and goes out in the process—are complementary aspects of the work that goes into forming and supporting a household.

A phrase sometimes used to describe the process of establishing such a partnership is "settling down." These days it is not a very popular phrase. "Settling down" sounds like something you do after your life has lost all its excitement. Our culture glorifies independence and mobility, not commitments and rootedness. And yet it is within the contexts of commitments and routines that individuals and families thrive. Building a marriage consists in part of settling into patterns that allow spouses to believe that together they are doing the best they can to earn enough money to meet their obligations, to manage that money appropriately, and to provide one another with a dependable and nurturing home life.

Making a Living

In modern American society, most careers, and the educational opportunities that lead to them, are open to persons of both sexes. Young men and women alike are encouraged to go to college, and to aspire to careers as varied as business or ministry, teaching or computer science or public service, law or medicine or engineering. Most people simply assume that all adults will both want and need to spend most of their lives in the paid work force, with the possible exception of some smaller or larger number of years devoted in full or in part to rearing children.

At the same time, however, there exists among some Christians a sense that supporting a family is properly a man's job, and that caring for a home and children is a woman's job. A good Christian husband supports his family single-handedly, or at least earns more money than his wife does. A good Christian wife puts her small salary in the bank, saving against the day when children arrive and she quits her job to stay home with them. Men belong in the workplace, maximizing their career potential; women belong in the home, caring for the family—and that is just the way things are and ought to be.

This notion actually owes far more to the process of industrialization than it does to any timeless arrangements set in place by God.[1] In the agricultural and artisanal economy that existed in this country through the middle of the nineteenth century, most men and women worked together in and around the home at a variety of interrelated tasks that while differentiated by gender— the cutting and carrying of wood by men, for example, and the building and tending of fires by women—were similar in that both were unwaged, and both contributed obviously and directly to the well-being of the household.

Industrialization changed that by removing a great deal of work from homes to factories, and by changing the nature of the work that remained in homes. After industrialization, men (and some women, mostly single) "went to work," that is, they left their homes in order to labor somewhere else for wages. Married women (who before the advent of reliable contraception tended frequently to be pregnant or nursing) "stayed home," where their infants and other children were, and where they continued to labor without pay, doing housework (which only increased in scope and intensity with the introduction of technological innovations like cookstoves and detergents).

Thus there emerged the notion that it is a man's job to go to work and to support a family, and a (married) woman's job to stay home and "not work." This "doctrine of separate spheres," as it is sometimes called, was comforting to some, as it seemed to soften the hard edges of the industrialized and market economy by guaranteeing that women would keep the fires of civilization burning at home. It was infuriating and suffocating to others, however, as it assigned many interesting occupations, and the money and status that went with them, exclusively to men, while relegating

---

[1]On this point and on the following discussion, see Ruth Schwartz Cowan, *More Work for Mother: The Ironies of Household Technology from the Open Hearth to the Microwave Oven* (New York: Basic, 1983).

women, and wives in particular, to what seemed lives of endless
unpaid servitude.

The feminist movement of the 1960s and 1970s was fueled in
part by the desire of many women to gain access to the same range
of occupations that were open to men. Although many disparities
of wage and rank still exist, this agenda has largely been accom-
plished, with very few occupations remaining in which women
are not represented. More recently, with the collapse of the industrial economy, the entrance of women into the workplace has ac-
celerated. The factory jobs that allowed at least some blue-collar
working men to support a family on one salary have all but disappeared, and the simultaneous explosion of housing and health
care costs have meant that many families, even frugal ones, find
that they simply must have two incomes just to make ends meet.

It is easy to see the attractions and benefits—and the necessity—
of paid work. Many professions involve obviously interesting and
engaging work, and even less-interesting jobs generate paychecks
that can be used to pay the bills. And in the secular, market-driven
model that dominates much of our society, it is now simply assumed
that economic well-being is best served when all adults work full
time for pay. A perhaps unforeseen result, however, is homes in
which no one has time to cook the meals or wash the clothes or
clean the house, and in which everyone, adults and children alike,
is equally starved for nurturance and care.[2]

In fact, the work involved in making a home is just as valuable
and necessary as the work involved in earning a paycheck. But the
preference voiced by some Christians, that wives stay home while
husbands earn paychecks, is much more problematic. Is it really
possible for most families in today's economy to manage details
like health insurance and mortgage payments and repayment of

---

[2]See, for example, Arlie Hochschild, *The Time Bind: When Work Becomes Home and
Home Becomes Work* (New York: Metropolitan Books, 1997).

educational debt on a single salary? Where is the justice in the assumption that only women's careers should be interrupted or sidetracked or indeed affected in any way by the needs of home and children? How can men participate in rearing their children if the burden of earning the family's money rests solely upon their shoulders? How can children experience their families in wholeness if one of their parents is never home?

Many Christian young people feel keenly the pressure placed on them by questions like these. Many women (especially) want very much to rear their own children and keep their own houses, and they worry that they will not be able to find a man who can support the family while they work less than full time or not at all. At the same time, most women have at least some interest in a career outside the home and want to find a way to have both that career and a satisfying life in the home and as a parent. They suspect strongly that this will require the support and active participation of their husbands, both in the home and with the children, possibly at some cost to the husbands' own careers. How likely, they wonder, is that to happen?

Young men have other worries: in particular, that they will not be able to earn enough money to support a family. They are in many cases looking forward to marriage and children, but they see their primary contribution to the family as an ability to support them financially. They then worry that they will not be able to do so, particularly if they are entering low-wage occupations like ministry or social service or teaching. If a man cannot support his family as a sole wage earner, they wonder, does this make him less of a man, or less of a Christian?

In fact, it is entirely possible for husbands and wives to order their marriages along Christian lines without having to conform to a pattern (that of the wage-earning husband and the stay-at-home wife) that belongs to a very specific cultural setting and that even in its heyday was never available to many people who were not wealthy or at least middle-class. It is similarly possible for husbands and wives to forge partnerships in which both parties are able to pursue satisfying work outside the home, while also sharing in care for one another and for their children at home.

But work and career arrangements that are satisfying to both spouses and that meet their needs for both money and nurturance do not happen automatically. Couples must work toward them intentionally and flexibly. You probably cannot have exactly what you want, or think you want, at least not right away or over the course of your entire marriage. This is true not least because what you need or want may change. Most people now change their jobs and even their careers over the course of their lives, sometimes because they want to, and sometimes because they have to. Married couples have to be prepared to deal with this, to change their own understandings of work and their arrangements with respect to work, as circumstances require.

This is not always easy to do. Career aspirations are often, and appropriately, a factor in decisions about whom to marry. One spouse agrees to earn enough money that the other can stay home with the children. One spouse agrees to put the other through graduate school first, and they agree that after that they will trade places. One or both spouses agree to pursue careers in fields that are not particularly exciting, because it seems that financial stability will be more attainable if they do so.

And then the ground shifts. The job or the salary they are counting on fails to materialize. A baby arrives unexpectedly and disrupts plans for school or work. One or the other spouse decides he or she just cannot stand to work a given job any longer, and wants to quit and pursue some old or newly discovered passion—perhaps one that is likely to change their financial circumstances for the worse, or to require a sacrifice of some kind from the other spouse.

Things like this can seem like betrayals, like one spouse has failed to live up to the bargain that he or she struck upon entering the marriage. "This is not what I signed up for!" the other spouse may think. Well, no, it may not be. But life is full of changes, many of which we don't ask for and may not see coming. The opportunity for a couple at points like this is to talk, to listen, to seek mutual understanding of their joint circumstances and desires, and then to strategize about possible alternatives or compromises that are acceptable to both of them, and that will allow them together to support one another and the rest of their household.

All work-related decisions come with tradeoffs. No ideal arrangement exists in which there are only gains and no losses for all concerned. Many jobs that offer family-friendly flexibility do not pay very well or offer no benefits. Many jobs with high earning potential require very long hours. Making time to rear children early in your career may mean that you will never advance as far as you might have, had you delayed having children. Waiting to have children may mean dealing with infertility, or having to take time away from a career that is just hitting its stride.[3]

As you consider what choices to make in ordering your work lives, do not underestimate the difficulty, costs and benefits involved in not being slaves to your (paid) jobs. We live in a culture in which the necessities of life (like housing, education and health care) are very expensive, and the options (nice clothes, nice cars, nice vacations) are even more expensive. Everything about our society encourages people to work as hard as they can, for as much money as they can, so they can spend as much as they possibly can.

In a context like this, it is very difficult to make choices that result in less income. But there is more to life than working to earn money. In particular, there is unpaid work to be done at

---

[3]For a discussion of work-life balance, see David Leonhardt, "Careers That Work for Families," *New York Times*, May 27, 2009.

home, in creating a nurturing family environment for your spouse, for your children, and for the guests who enter your home. Fathers, in particular, are prone to forget this. "My father's main focus in life is to make sure there is enough money for the family to stay afloat," wrote one man. "He has never really concerned himself with getting involved with his kids or shaping our characters. I realize I know next to nothing about him. He was just always the guy who got up really early and came home after I had left for the evening."

This young man, and many like him, are very thankful for the faithful financial support that their fathers gave their families. But they mourn the loss of any meaningful relationship with fathers who were always at work. Children need time with both of their parents, and spouses need time with one another. Deciding to work less for pay and to share work at home can be one of the best investments a husband and a wife make together. You may have to live more modestly than some others do. In a society that reckons a family's value by how much money they have or seem to have, that is not a trivial loss. But in return you may gain a much richer and more stable family life, precisely because you have taken the time to nurture one another.

Keeping the Books

Money matters. In a monetary economy, money marks the difference between people who have what they need and people who don't. In a consumer society, entire industries—namely, advertising and credit—exist solely to fan the desire for money and the things money can buy. And even in societies and economies very different from our own, people have craved money and the power and status conferred by money, to the point that they have had to be warned against the dangers of making money into an idol: as Jesus says, "you cannot serve both God and Money" (Matthew 6:24 NIV).

Some Christians have decided that the best way to follow Jesus is to have no money at all. Like Saint Francis, they have sought to live in "apostolic poverty," imitating Jesus, who had no place to lay his head, and Jesus' disciples, who went out without purse or bag or sandals to preach the coming of the kingdom of God (Luke 9:58; 10:4). Apostolic poverty has been a subject of fierce controversy among Christians, in large part because of the uncomfortable questions it raises about the wealth of individual Christians and of the church as a whole. Didn't Jesus say that it was easier for a camel to pass through the eye of a needle than for a rich person to enter the kingdom of heaven (Mark 10:25)? Doesn't this suggest that the advocates of apostolic poverty have a point, and that "riches" (however defined) are an obstacle to salvation?

The desire to maintain that salvation and wealth are mutually compatible has given rise to a considerable amount of creative interpretation of this text and of the many other passages in Scripture that speak of money, of poverty, and of material well-being.[4] Regardless of the merits of these interpretations, the fact is that most Christians have not sworn off money. Most Christians have lived in the midst of whatever economic system has prevailed in

---

[4]Some modern interpreters have suggested that the reference in Mark 10:25 is not to a camel (Greek *kamēlon*) but to a rope (Greek *kamilon*), the point thus being that just as it is difficult (but not impossible) for a rope to pass through the eye of a needle, it is difficult (but not impossible) for a rich person to be saved. Another suggestion, dating from the Middle Ages, is that the "Needle's Eye" was a narrow gate in Jerusalem which could be entered by a camel only with difficulty. For these options, see Craig A. Evans, *Mark 8:27–16:20*, Word Biblical Commentary 34b (Nashville: Thomas Nelson, 2001), p. 101. Ancient interpreters suggest variously that Jesus is warning not against the possession of wealth per se but against excessive desire for or attachment to wealth (Clement of Alexandria), that the salvation of the wealthy is possible because God makes it possible (Origen), that Jesus is calling all people, including the rich, to careful stewardship (Jerome), that it is not riches themselves but one's inner disposition toward them that matters (Augustine), that it is a good idea for the rich to divest themselves gradually of possessions, or at least of the desire for more and superfluous possessions (John Chrysostom). See Christopher A. Hall, *Reading Scripture with the Church Fathers* (Downers Grove, Ill.: InterVarsity Press, 1998), pp. 170-76.

their time and place, and have tried—with varying degrees of success—to live faithfully within whatever financial constraints and opportunities have come their way.

For some people, this has meant wrestling with the implications of wealth. For others, it has meant making do with less—sometimes much less—than many others. For everyone, it means making a variety of decisions about how to manage money: how to earn it, how to spend it, how much to save, how much to give, whether to borrow, how to repay debts incurred. And it means making all these decisions in the context of the families and larger communities in which we find ourselves. Money and the management of money are never purely private concerns. Our decisions and our desires necessarily affect our relationships and the people with whom we are in relationship.

All this is complex, and so perhaps it is understandable that people would seek ways to make it simpler. One way to do that is to suppose that there are special Christian rules for money management which, if followed, will guarantee financial success. Sometimes tithing is seen as the key practice. "I was taught that as long as you tithe, everything else will work itself out," wrote one woman. Sometimes the key is a shared checking account (symbolizing mutual commitment to the marriage), or reliance on the husband's income alone (symbolizing a commitment to "biblical" gender roles), or the avoidance of debt (symbolizing virtuous self-reliance and rejection of over-consumption).

We have our doubts. Tithing is a time-honored Christian practice, and so is a willingness to share one's financial resources with others both inside and outside the Christian community; but tithing and generosity are like other kinds of Christian virtue, in that sometimes they have tangible benefits for those who practice them, and sometimes they don't. A husband and wife should of course be mutually committed to their marriage, and shared finances can be an expression of such a commitment; but it is imaginable that some genuinely committed couples might under certain circumstances find separate or partially separate bank accounts necessary or simply desirable.

Reliance on a husband's earnings alone is a bourgeois ideal, not a Christian one; it has its roots not in the Bible but in the industrial revolution. And while avoidance of debt is a good thing in the abstract, some people who get into intractable debt do so not because they are weak or greedy, but because they are poor or sick or disabled and cannot afford the necessities of life, and neither the government nor the church nor any individual has offered them the kind of meaningful assistance that might have allowed them to pay for things like housing and food and medical care and education while also staying out of debt.

The wise and Christian management of money is in fact a prudential matter. It involves very few rights and wrongs, and many matters of judgment. You need a basic knowledge of how money works: how to balance a checkbook, how to read a bank statement, how to make a budget. You also need to know the specifics of your own financial situation: your income, your expenses, your assets, your liabilities.[5]

Beyond this, you need to work together with your spouse or prospective spouse to make appropriate decisions about money and to follow through on those decisions in your day-to-day saving and spending and giving. Doing these things well often has less to do with money itself than it has to do with relational habits like honesty, consideration, and a willingness to acknowledge and work with each other's strengths and experiences and personal style.

---

[5]One place to start is with the website of the National Association of Personal Financial Advisors <www.napfa.org> which includes consumer information related to financial planning, the choice of a financial advisor, and books on financial planning.

Money often acts as a kind of magnifying glass, taking dynamics or tendencies that are present in the partners or in the relationship as a whole and amplifying them. Negative patterns of relationship that might otherwise seem negligible can become pressing and even overwhelming when the issue at hand is money. On the other hand, if when relational issues surface in the context of money management, you take the opportunity to deal with them intentionally and constructively, the benefits of doing so can extend far beyond your financial situation, as you learn increasingly to trust one another and to work together as a team.

In almost every relationship, there is one partner who grew up with more money and one who grew up with less, one partner who is more of a spender and one who is more of a saver, one who worries more and one who worries less, one who likes to plan ahead and track details and one who is more a free spirit and a big-picture person. It can take time to identify your differences and to find ways to draw on them as mutually complementary strengths.

There are a number of potential pitfalls to avoid when dealing with money. Don't be silent about money. Money is not a secret, and treating it as if it were gives it the wrong kind of power. Silence imparts a kind of quasi-magical aura to money, making it seem at once less real and more threatening than it really is. But while speechless awe is appropriate before God, money requires straightforward conversation.

So talk about it. Perhaps you grew up with plenty and are worried about how you will react to being a newlywed on a budget. Perhaps you grew up on food stamps and are worried that a similar degree of financial insecurity could mark your adulthood. Talk about your current financial situation—your level of indebtedness or savings, your patterns of earning and spending. Perhaps you feel confident about your situation; perhaps you feel frightened or embarrassed or uncertain. Whatever the particulars, it is important to share them with one another so that you can begin to deal with them together.

Don't hide behind money. Money is not—or should not be—a mask behind which you fight about other things without naming what those things are. There is hardly anything that cannot be turned into a fight about money—whose family is the better one, whose contribution to the household is more important, who is the more considerate, the more thoughtful, the more carefree, the more responsible, the more important, the more virtuous.

The chance is slim that fighting about any of these things behind the mask of money is going to do anything either to improve your financial situation or to address whatever the underlying conflict is about. So if conversations about money seem to veer weirdly out of control, take the hint and ask: What's really going on here? It may take some time to figure it out, and more time to build together habits of talking about one subject at a time and being honest about what that subject is. But it will be much easier in the end to manage your money well if you can disentangle financial issues from others, and deal with them separately and directly.

Don't use money as a weapon. In our society, as in most others, money, status and power go together. Thus the temptation is ever present to use money as a means of asserting or raising one's own status, or of wielding power against others. Sometimes this is attempted through secret-keeping—the husband who cashes his paycheck and hands his wife an allowance, so she cannot know how much he earns or how much he has kept for himself; the wife who goes shopping and then smuggles the packages into the house in the hope that she will be able to keep her husband from knowing how much she bought. Sometimes people attempt to wield power with threats: "Earn more money, or I will despise you." "Spend less money, or I will leave you." And sometimes control is simply seized, as when one partner makes significant financial decisions or purchases without consulting the other: a house, a boat, a car, a loan, an investment.

Threats and secrets and unilateral actions can be effective, in the sense that they do affect the balance of power in relationships. But they destroy trust and any semblance of mutuality or coresponsibility. The temptation to seize power, whether openly or underhandedly, can be a strong one, but it is essentially a vote of no confidence in the relationship. If you want your marriage not only to survive but to thrive, you have to choose the harder route of working openly and cooperatively with one another, in financial matters as much—or more—as in any other dimension of the relationship.

And finally, don't play with money. Contrary to what Las Vegas, Wall Street and Madison Avenue would like us all to believe, money is not a toy. Money is a tool, and the pleasure in using a tool comes from using it skillfully and appropriately. So whether your inclination is to fritter away your money at the gaming table, in speculative investments, or on clothes or video games, take a deep breath and think about whether there is money in the budget for such things.

Of course this assumes that you have a budget. It assumes that you know how much money you have, that you have set aside sums for saving and for giving and for paying bills, and that you know whether there are discretionary funds left over for you to spend as you please. If there are, by all means, go ahead. It is fine to spend money on things that you believe will give you pleasure. The fact that money is a tool does not mean you must only spend it on things that are drab and utilitarian. It does mean that "fun" purchases need to be made with money you have, not with money you don't.

Money management is not just a necessity, and not just a challenge. Money management is an opportunity to live in the real world, to tell the truth, to acknowledge both the limitations and the possibilities of your circumstances, to order your priorities, to consider others, and to share what you have with your spouse, your children, your family and friends, and with the larger community of worthwhile causes and needy acquaintances and strangers.

Money management is also a parable. It forms a microcosm of how you see yourself, your spouse, your marriage, the rest of God's world and God himself. People too easily fix on money as the ultimate source of security, whether they have it (and want to make sure they don't lose it) or whether they don't (and wish they did). Money can be put to all kinds of good uses, and there are all kinds of scary possibilities that go along with not having enough. But in the last analysis, money cannot keep you safe. Only God can do that, and our job as human beings—and as husbands and wives, if we are married—is to keep faith with one another, and do the best we can with what we have.

Making a Home

One young woman shared the following story:

> I got back to my apartment after my evening class exhausted and starving. I started making myself dinner. Then my boyfriend came over. He was carrying a packet of microwave macaroni and cheese. After greeting him, I went back to the kitchen to continue making my dinner. He followed me. "Honey," he said, in that tone of voice that means he wants me to do something. "Could you make me some macaroni and cheese?" "Why can't you do it?" I replied. He answered, "Because I want you to do it." Visions of me with a handkerchief around my head on my hands and knees scrubbing a floor with a baby on my back flooded my mind. He knew I had had a long day and I was in the middle of making myself

the first meal I'd eaten that day, and he expected me to make
him his stupid microwave macaroni and cheese?

Why is housework such an emotional and relational minefield?
One set of reasons has to do with the expectations that people
bring to housework. One typical expectation is that women will
do housework, and men will not. "The traditional Christian wife
portrayed in my church was a loving mother who always cooked,
took care of the kids, did the laundry, and cleaned the house,"
wrote a young man. "The husband would spend his days at work
'making the money,' and would come home to a wonderful dinner
prepared by his wife, followed by a relaxing evening on the couch."
"I had this vision of my husband sitting in a chair with his feet up
and me running around serving him hand and foot," wrote a new
bride. "This was my vision of a good wife."

What's wrong with this? In the first place, this ideal leads to
vastly different outcomes for men and for women. If only the husband goes out to work, the result is that when he is at work, he is
working, and when he is at home, he is resting. The result for his
wife is that her work is at home, and since she is always at home,
she is always working. So when does she rest? Even God rests.
Shouldn't wives be allowed to do the same? And if both husband
and wife go out to work (as in our culture virtually all husbands
and wives do before they have children, and sometimes afterward
as well), the husband comes home from work to rest, and the wife
comes home from work to more work. So again—when does she
rest? When does she come "home," to a place prepared for her,
where someone nurtures and cares for her instead of expecting
her to labor incessantly for others?

In the second place, the archetypes of the "good wife" (whose
manic eagerness to do it all herself results only in good for her and
for her family) and of her presumed counterpart, the "good hus-

band" (whose domestic passivity is somehow likewise just as good for everyone) exist only in the realm of the imagination. What exists in real life is a collection of much more mixed characters, some of them genuinely unsavory. Roles commonly occupied by women include the maid of all work (who is worn to a frazzle by her service to a family that never lifts a finger to help her), the passive-aggressive martyr (who shows her anger over the unequal division of household chores by refusing to tell her husband what he could do to contribute), the domestic dictator (who insists that anyone who helps has to do it her way) and the smothering mother (whose insistence on doing everything for everyone prevents her husband and children from taking appropriate responsibility for themselves or for the family).

On the masculine side, there is the lord of the manor (who thinks it is only fair that his wife should do all the work around the house, because he earns more money than she does—never mind the fact that she works just as many hours outside the home as he does), the well-meaning bumbler (whose idea of helping out is to go outside and rake leaves in peaceful solitude, while his wife wrestles indoors with the vacuum cleaner, the toilet brush and the children), the technological hermit (who comes home from work to sit in front of the computer for the remainder of the evening, all the while assuming that hot meals and clean clothes will just appear out of nowhere) and the lazy bum (who sits on the couch in front of the television and orders the children to help their mother but never lifts a finger himself).

It doesn't have to be this way. And in some households, it isn't. In some households, housework is both performed and received as a faithful expression of love made visible. Those who do the housework at least sometimes enjoy the work itself, finding pleasure in turning piles of dirty laundry into baskets of neatly folded clothes, transforming an untidy house into a neat and clean one, cooking a tasty and nutritious meal, setting an attractive table on a weeknight and a sparkling one on a holiday. And those who benefit from housework appreciate it and find ways to participate in it. They enjoy coming home and being at home; they learn to notice what has been done and what needs doing, and to enter willingly into the rhythms of the household and the work that keeps it going.

What makes the difference? What can couples and individuals do to help themselves end up, not in the land of the unhappy stereotypes of overworked wives and chore-shirking husbands, but in a place where housework becomes the matrix of a shared and happy daily life? Reckoning honestly with gender-based formation concerning home and housework can be a place to begin. Men and women tend to be socialized very differently where these things are concerned. Men are typically socialized—whether by their families, by the church or by the culture at large—simply to assume that housework is "not my job." In the words of one man: "When you asked, 'Who takes care of things in your house?' the only answer I could think of was, 'Not me.'"

This young man hailed from a family in which both parents did housework and required the children to help—and he had still arrived at young adulthood with the sense that it was his job to take orders, but someone else's job to take charge.

> I've never given much thought to what I want my home to be like. When I moved into the dorm my freshman year, I just dumped my stuff around the room in a semi-orderly manner. When I moved into an apartment senior year, I did the same. My living space just sort of "happens," without any premeditation. I think that's how I've been planning to proceed. I always figured that once I got married, my wife would take care of all that.

We have never heard a woman say anything remotely like this. Women are socialized to think about their homes, to care about them, to believe that housework is their responsibility, and to believe that their housekeeping is a direct reflection of their value as women and as wives. Even women who don't really believe these things often feel a kind of guilty sense that they should, or that other people think they should. As a result, for good or ill, housework carries a great deal of emotional freight in the lives of many, if not most, women. Sometimes they want to keep house just the way their mothers did. Sometimes they want to keep house just the way they wish their mothers had. And they are very often inclined to view their opinions about housekeeping as the final word on how things ought to be done, and to doubt that anyone else can really do the job right, at least not without a great deal of instruction and supervision.

These asymmetric expectations concerning house and home are among the reasons why many couples find it a challenge to learn to share the housekeeping. If he has been trained not to notice or to care about what needs doing, and she has been trained to believe it is her job to do it and only she can do it adequately, then she is not going to be inclined to let go of the work, and he is not going to be inclined to take it on. But there are good reasons to make the effort to share both the work itself and control over it and responsibility for it.

One reason is that housekeeping is too big a job to be assigned exclusively to a spouse who has any other job, whether that be child rearing or paid work outside the home. Another reason is that housework offers the only opportunity many couples have to do tangible, physical work together. Most husbands and wives spend their work days separately, with evenings and weekends as their only time together. Sharing some of that time as leisure can be important, but sharing some of it as work is at least as important. This is your chance to accomplish something together, to build a home, to create an environment of order and beauty and mutual service and dependable daily routines that over time will form the substance of your shared life.

There are as many ways to share the housework as there are couples to share it. You have to figure out what works for you. If you are both the type who believe that many hands make light work, you might choose to do all or many of the chores together. If you like more independence while you work, you might rather divvy up the chores. You could base your division of labor on who knows how to do what—perhaps one of you is an experienced cook, and the other has had more practice cleaning. Maybe you like doing different things—one of you likes to do the dishes, the other likes to do the laundry. Maybe one of you is home from work earlier than the other. If so, it would make sense for him or her to cook the dinner, or at least do the prep work, and for the other to clean up afterward.

Ideally, some of these possible ways of sharing the work will correspond to what you as individuals already like and want to do. It is harder when neither of you likes to clean but the cleaning still needs to be done, or when the spouse who gets home first and is thus available to cook dinner is the one who has never learned to cook or doesn't like to cook. Now is when you really have the opportunity to figure out how to work together. Talk about it; identify what needs doing, what ideas each of you has about how to get it done and what solutions might work for both of you.

Whatever you do, don't treat issues related to housekeeping as of little account. Things like who cleans the bathroom (and what counts as cleaning the bathroom) may seem like small details, but they have the capacity to grow into sources of enormous resentment if they are not clarified and dealt with in ways that make both spouses feel like partners whose preferences and labor are equally valued. This doesn't mean you have to agree about everything—one or both of you may always feel that the other is overly meticulous, or not nearly meticulous enough. It does mean that each of you needs to feel that the other is making a good-faith effort to contribute to the work of the household, and that your own contributions are noticed and appreciated.

Above all, remember that if you want to have a home, you have to make a home. "There is not a single thing about my current apartment that I'll miss when I'm gone," wrote one man. "On the other hand, there are plenty of things from my old house that I miss all the time." Why the difference? He had never done a thing to make his apartment a home, he realized, whereas his parents had devoted a great deal of time and effort to making the house he grew up in a home for themselves and for their children. Maybe, it occurred to him, he should make an effort to learn to keep house. "Maybe I'll discover some talents and passions that I never knew were there. And even if housework never thrills me, at least I'll be practicing an intentional love for my family."

Settling Down

You can learn a lot about the modern American worldview by asking people what their financial goals are. Chances are, the word *vacation* will come up. What are people saving for? A car, or maybe a vacation. A down payment on a house, or a vacation. Paying down educational or credit-card debt, or a vacation. Retirement, or a vacation.

What is going on here? How is it that purely optional extras—like vacations—can even be mentioned in the same breath as basic budget items like transportation, housing, debt repayment and retirement savings? What is going on is that people don't think of vacations as extras. They think of them as a basic element of the good life. In the cultural setting in which we live, travel is good and staying in one place is bad. How do you know you have a life? You take a vacation.

No wonder it is so hard for us to keep our commitments. We make them easily enough—after all, when you first commit to something, it is new and exciting and seemingly full of endless possibilities. But sticking with something over the long haul is harder. It starts to seem like the same old grind, filled now not with possibilities but with routine, with duty, with sameness. So we want to escape; we want to get away; we want a vacation.

There is nothing wrong with wanting change. But you don't necessarily have to go on vacation to get it, and you don't have to break your commitments in order not to be suffocated with boredom. On the contrary—some of the most deeply satisfying possibilities that life offers are found not by breaking commitments but by keeping them. Some of the very best kinds of change are not the abrupt changes that you encounter by getting on a plane to somewhere else, but the gradual changes that can be entered into only by patient faithfulness to a particular place, particular people, a particular relationship.

Establishing a household—what our grandparents used to call settling down—begins with planning and decisions: where to live, what jobs to pursue, how to make ends meet, how to keep the house. Then there is lots of work to do in making that all happen, and in making changes when the original plans either don't work out or run their course and need to be succeeded by whatever comes next. And it all takes time—time to establish where you are, to decide where you'd like to be, to work toward that place, to get to know one another better as you do.

The pleasure of settling down is not only in the product but in the process. Little by little, your life together will emerge, small and promising at first, then more and more substantial, and eventually mature and bearing fruit. Each stage has its own pleasures and challenges; at each point there are things to do and things to enjoy. It takes work, and sustained attention and presence—and it brings with it a richness and depth that can be had no other way.

9

Old Love

Growing Together into Maturity

WHAT HAPPENS AFTER THE WEDDING? In a fairy tale, nothing, or virtually nothing. The prince and princess live happily ever after. We don't get any details, not even about the honeymoon, let alone where they decide to live and where they get jobs and how they decide to celebrate the holidays. In a fairy tale, the wedding is not just the climax of the story; it is the end of the story. Once the bridal couple walks down the aisle, the last noteworthy event of their lives has happened; the curtain closes and the story is over.

Real life is much more interesting than this. In real life, the wedding is not the end; it is the beginning—or at least *a* beginning. Young love exists precisely for the purpose of growing into old love. That is not to say that young love is not a wonderful and worthwhile thing in itself. But young love is to old love as the seed is to the flower or the tree. It is a small beginning, pregnant with possibilities that with time and care have the potential to grow into something much more complex and substantial than they yet are.

This truth is not always easy to see in our culture, which is obsessed with youth and assumes that getting older is a disaster in every respect. In such a culture, the tendency is to believe that a good marriage is one in which both the partners and their relationship remain perpetually young. The sort of breathless infatuation that most often characterizes very young people in very new relationships is taken as representing the pinnacle of intimate attachment, and the job of people who want to be happily married is then defined as remaining perpetually in that state.

Christian Scripture and tradition teach us otherwise. In a Christian understanding, growing old is not a catastrophe; it is a blessing. To grow old in the company of a husband or wife of many years is to be doubly blessed. There is more to life, and to marriage, than the first blush of young love. There is, to be specific, old love—or at least older love, love that has begun to mature and to take on a greater gravity than it had at first.

Love does not always mature. We all know couples whose marriages have not survived, or have not developed in ways that are positive and life-giving. But many marriages do thrive. Many couples do grow into old love. "Each time I see my grandparents, I walk away more amazed by their wisdom and love for life, family, and most importantly, each other," wrote one young man. "The other day my grandfather cracked a joke, and as she was laughing my grandmother reached over and touched his arm. You could tell there was love in her touch."

What does it take to grow into a love like this? Of course there is no formula that can be mechanically applied to every couple in every situation. People are different, and their stories develop differently. But certain habits of mind and heart and body can contribute to the deepening and maturing of marital relationships. Among these are the formation of appropriate and helpful expectations of married life, the sharing of traditions, and the bearing together of the difficulties and sorrows that are inevitably a part of life, including married life. As practices like these are lived together, love matures and bears the fruit of joy, stability and peace.

Expectations

It is natural to have expectations of marriage. Part of the reason people get married is that they expect that certain desirable things will happen if they do. Some expectations make life easier, by helping us to know what to look for, priming us to be grateful for good things when they occur, and preparing us to meet challenges when they arise. Other expectations make life harder, by encouraging us to want the impossible and setting us up for inevitable disappointment when the impossible does not, in fact, transpire.

A few months into her marriage, one young woman began to realize that she had walked down the aisle with an expectation of the second sort, namely, that her marriage would be perfect.

> I was in love! I had been swept off my feet, and I was going to live the rest of my life in a fairy-tale world in which I would always be adored, cherished and loved. My husband would never disagree with me, because I would always be right. If an issue did arise, we would settle it by talking for hours over coffee, never raising our voices or getting frustrated with one another. We would conclude our conversation with a hug and a kiss while thanking each other for the brilliant perspective. Then we would go home and make love.

It wasn't working out that way. Her marriage was not all candlelit lovemaking amidst rose petals on white satin sheets. Her husband didn't always want to go shopping with her on a Sunday afternoon rather than watching the game. He didn't always compliment her on her cooking. And she didn't always have control of the remote! Puzzled, she talked with her mother. What had her mother's expectations been of her dad when she married him? Had they been fulfilled? Her mother's response: she had not been disappointed by anything. All her expectations had been fulfilled. "I couldn't believe it," the daughter wrote. "I mean, how could my mother be married to the one perfect guy on the planet?"

As they talked, more of the story came out. The mother had grown up in an unstable and abusive home, "dreaming not of a big wedding with a puffy white dress and thousands of pink roses, but of a peaceful home with a kind, responsible man. Her expectations were, 'Don't beat me up, don't cheat on me, and always put God, me and the kids first.'" The man she married had done all these things. Years later, their children almost raised, they were still together, still thankful for one another, still very much in love.

This young woman's parents had built a stable and happy marriage, not because either of them was perfect or expected perfection from the other, but because they desired from one another and gave to one another the kindness and respect that each of them wanted and deserved. Their most significant expectations of one another had been focused on fundamentals, and they had not been disappointed.

There are other expectations that can help you anticipate and rise to some of the challenges and opportunities of marriage. Expect that the process of getting to know your partner will continue after you are married. This will be true no matter how well you know each other when you marry. It may seem, while you are still in the midst of the first bloom of love, that your partner can read your mind and understand your very being. In fact, he or she cannot, and you have got a lot to learn about him or her as well.

How can we be so sure? Because getting married changes things. The very commitment that marriage represents makes it possible for spouses to perceive one another and to reveal themselves to one another in new and deeper ways. If you are psychologically healthy people in a basically sound relationship, what you learn about your partner after the wedding will be consonant with what you knew about him or her before your marriage. But there will be more of it, and it will be more complex and interesting than you could have imagined. The process of getting to know one another does not end with the wedding; instead, it enters a new phase.

The passage of time also changes what there is to know. People grow and change, and their knowledge of each other needs to grow and change as well. This happens before marriage, and it happens over the life span of a marriage. You may have truly understood your partner last week or last month or last year, but you are not therefore done with getting to know him or her. You have to allow for the possibility that some of what you know about your spouse may need to change or develop, even as your spouse and your marriage are changing and developing.

Change is itself something to expect. Change occupies a complicated place in our culture, particularly where romantic relationships are concerned. Fairy tales and youth culture both encourage us to believe that such relationships are at their peak the moment the partners say, "I do." If this is so, where is there to go but down? We therefore fear change, assuming that if things change, they will do so for the worse.

At the same time, though, we assume that any degree of stability equals an equal degree of boredom. It really doesn't seem possible to make an enduring commitment and still have an interesting life. As one man wrote: "How can you be sure that all of life is not the same?" The permanence of marriage can seem akin to having your life set in concrete, with no possibility that anything new or exciting will ever happen again.

In fact, change is inevitable, even in the context of a permanent commitment like marriage. No one stands still in life; no relationship can remain unchanged over time. Christians believe that change is purposive and directed toward a goal, namely, the kingdom of God. And if history is moving toward a goal, then so are people, whether married or not. The question is not whether your marriage will change, but how it will change, and what the nature of those changes will be.

Some change does come with loss. If something is good and it changes, then that particular good no longer exists. But a great deal of change is not so much either good or bad as it is simply different. There is a difference between buying a house when your children are babies, fixing up the house when they are school age, and seeing them married in the backyard when they are adults. Who is to say that any one of these stages is better than another? They are simply different; each has its own challenges and its own joys, and your privilege as husband and wife is to encounter these things together and to share in them with one another.

Of course, people can sometimes change in ways that make them less rather than more able to live peaceably and contentedly together. One challenge of marriage lies in changing together in ways that are increasingly positive and interrelated, rather than increasingly distant and alienated. The busyness and the technological clutter of contemporary American culture are forces that push people apart, encouraging us to spend our time rushing from place to place, sitting down only in front of television and computer screens, interacting with other people mostly at a distance and by pushing buttons.

When we do this, the change that is inevitably a part of human life comes to us in isolation, and we may find after not too much time has gone by that we hardly know each other and no longer care to do so. If we want to change together, we have to cultivate community. We have to eat together and work together and talk together, and allow ourselves to be changed by and with one another.

The importance of community in marriage points toward another significant expectation: expect that people other than your marital partner will play key roles in your marriage. In the contemporary myth of romance, marriage is just about the two of you, and other people are simply beside the point. As one person writes, "I was under the impression that marriage was the 'relationship of all relationships,' and that once you were married, other people would naturally fall by the wayside."

In fact, people need each other. Their desires for relationship, for support and for companionship are too great and too varied to be met solely by a husband or by a wife. A spouse is a very important person, but he or she cannot possibly be everything to you. Friendships can nourish and strengthen a marriage relationship by allowing spouses the opportunity for give and take outside the relationship. It can actually be easier to appreciate all that a spouse is to you if there are other, different people in your life as well.

Marriage does change relationships. Friendships are altered when one of the parties marries. Family relationships change too. No longer are you just one of the guys, or just one of the girls; no longer just a son or a daughter. You are a husband or a wife, and this will inevitably reorder your priorities. You and your spouse will need to be intentional about making time for friends and family, and for cultivating those relationships in ways that complement and support your marriage.

Among the people who will play the most significant parts in your married life will be your children, should you have the opportunity to welcome children. Whether you foster or adopt or have your own, your children will arrive in your home as the individuals they are, and they will change you. When they get old enough they will invite their friends over, and the friends will change you too. This process will almost certainly not be entirely comfortable—but it can be enormously rewarding and enriching.

And perhaps one day your daughter will say, "When my friends meet my parents, they always say how amazing they are. I can see how much my parents have learned from the experiences my brother and I have brought to the family. I hope I have that same ability to be able to learn from my children when they are young and when they are grown, to not hold tightly to my perception of the way things should be when presented with a new and different way of thinking. I hope I will be willing to listen and learn, as my parents have been."

Other adults can be particularly important when challenges or difficulties present themselves, as they inevitably will. Not everyone is a good confidant. But there are people who can keep a confidence, who can listen in ways that are helpful, who can want the best for both of you, and can resist taking sides or passing judgment. The point of confiding in a friend about the challenges in your marriage is not to complain or to blame or vilify your spouse. The point is to gain some perspective on what is going on in your relationship, and find resources that can help you move forward.

So cultivate relationships, individually and as a couple, with a wide range of people. Make a point of speaking positively about your spouse to others. And when you have problems that you are facing together or that are disrupting your relationship with one another, talk with someone wise and empathetic about it. This might be a peer; it might be a parent or other relative, or an older person from church; it might be a pastor or a professional counselor. You need these other people in your life; they can help you make your marriage a success and a joy.

Expect, too, that each of you will need time alone. The pleasures of intimate relationship, and the high value that both secular and Christian culture place on finding a romantic partner, can encourage people to lose track of themselves in the midst of their relationships. But even a married person still has a self, and that self still needs time to rest and breathe and grow.

So don't try to construct a life or a relationship in which you do absolutely everything together. Give yourself room to be yourself, by yourself, and give your spouse the same. Most people need at least a little "me" time even when they are lovestruck newlyweds, and by the time there are several small children in the house and never a moment's peace from dawn to dusk, virtually everyone does. Find a corner of the house where you can read a book or keep a journal; set aside fifteen minutes to take a walk or ride your bicycle; offer to supervise the kids for a few minutes while your spouse does the same. You will feel better for it, and your marriage will feel better too.

Traditions

In the Christian life, everything you do gains its significance in part from its place in a broad and complex web of tradition. This is true of things that happen once in any given life: you are baptized once and confirmed once, and each of these events is a significant milestone in your pilgrimage of faith, as you join the countless others who have entered into these rituals of faith before you.

And then there are the many things that you do more than once: Sunday worship, private prayer, service projects, financial giving, participation in the feasts and fasts and liturgies associated with the Christian year—Advent, Christmas, Epiphany, Lent, Easter, Pentecost. Some of these events and activities may be memorable, and others may be less so, and taken together they constitute the fabric of which your Christian life is woven.

So also in married life. You get married once, and as you do you make promises and enter upon commitments that have shaped the lives of countless other couples before you. And then there are the many little things that you and your spouse do more than once, whether daily, weekly or yearly, and that over time will weave the web of tradition that forms your married life.

People cannot help but have traditions. None of us is creative enough to think of a new way to do something every time a particular circumstance arises. And for the most part, we don't want to. We want to know what to expect; we want to have something we can count on. So we settle on some way of doing things, we do it that way more than once, and before we realize, it has become a tradition, and we can hardly think of doing it any other way.

No two families' traditions are the same, a fact that shows itself particularly around the holidays. One woman told a story about the first fall that she was married. As the end of November approached, she reminded her husband to ask for Thanksgiving off. He replied that he was planning to ask if he could work Thanksgiving. She wrote,

> I was shocked. I couldn't imagine how he could possibly want to work on our first Thanksgiving together. I was so upset. I thought, "Holidays are not important to him. Family is not important to him. I am not important to him." Many tears and a long talk later, I came to learn that Thanksgiving had never been a big family holiday for his family. Some years they had not even spent it together. He didn't mean to upset me. He knew that we needed the extra money, and he just didn't value the holiday like I did.

The next month, they traveled across the country to spend Christmas with his family.

> I helped his mother pick out the Christmas tree, and later the whole family gathered around the tree to put on the ornaments they had each collected over the years. My husband asked where his ornaments were. "At home with the rest of the Christmas decorations," I said. He was devastated. It was

the first year he wasn't able to put his ornaments on his family's tree. I had no idea that it was a tradition. In my family we all sat on the couch and watched my mom decorate the tree.

As this young couple was beginning to discover, traditions do not only function as elements of continuity. Traditions change. Sometimes traditions need to change. Not all habits are good, after all, and even good habits sometimes outlive their usefulness. If your Italian immigrant family still has the dinner of the seven fishes on Christmas Eve, even though no one currently living either likes fish or enjoys the meal, it might be time to make a switch to spaghetti and meatballs.

At other times traditions have to change, because life has changed. People have married, or changed jobs, or moved house. As much as they might like to carry on as they have always done, they can't, because things are different now. Even when life changes are welcome, the loss of traditions associated with the way things used to be can be a significant sorrow. "I have realized that Christmas Eve and Easter with my parents will never be the same," wrote an engaged man. "There is a feeling of loss that I never expected to feel."

Thanksgiving and Christmas loom particularly large in the experience of many newlyweds. People tend to have many memories and many fond associations built up around these occasions. And the families of both the bride and groom often take a proprietary interest in the new couple and desire their attendance at family holiday celebrations. It can be hard for all concerned to make room for everyone to have preferences about how the holidays are celebrated, and to negotiate an arrangement that is good for everyone.

As you consider how to celebrate major holidays in your first few years of marriage, remember: you only have to decide one year at a time. We think in this regard of a story told by one engaged couple. He was very fond of his family's Thanksgiving traditions; she was very fond of her family's Christmas traditions. They decided that when they were married, they would like to spend Thanksgiving with his family and Christmas with hers. As a private preference, this might have been fine; but they happened to mention in passing to the groom's mother that they were planning to celebrate every Christmas of their married life with the bride's family. This did not go over well. They would have done better, they belatedly realized, to make and communicate their plans one year at a time, thus leaving room for both their own and their extended families' feelings and traditions to evolve.

Some families are able to make transitions more gracefully than others. It may be that among your relatives are some who are going to do their best to make you feel guilty if you don't give them everything they want and more. This will be an opportunity for you and your spouse to work together to figure out what some workable options are and which of your families' expectations and desires you can meet and which you cannot.

This, too, will be the beginning of a tradition of sorts. Is the holiday tradition that you get all bent out of shape trying to placate all your relatives, and end up resentful both of them and of each other? Or is the holiday tradition that you work together to come up with a plan that is as satisfying as you can manage, and then you have a warm and enjoyable holiday season with each other and with as many of your extended family as you end up seeing?

At least as important as holiday traditions are the many smaller habits that shape the days and weeks and seasons of a given family's life. Family game nights, bedtime prayers and lullabies, road trips, weekend picnics, hiking expeditions, riding with Dad in the car or behind him on the tractor, quilting or gardening with Mom, celebrations of birthdays and anniversaries and good report cards—these and many others are among traditions that can become significant threads in the fabric of your common life.

Traditions associated with meals and mealtime exercise a particularly formative influence on the lives of individuals and families. Meals happen several times a day, every single day, and the way we eat therefore occupies a central role in shaping who we are, individually and together. The combination of busyness and so-called convenience foods can result too easily in families in which most meals are eaten standing up by the microwave, with no opportunity for pleasure in either the food or each other.

With even a little planning and effort, a radically different scenario can transpire, one in which meals are prepared for one another and shared with one another. You don't have to spend a lot of money or fix fancy recipes in order to sit down to breakfast or dinner together. You do have to take the time to plan what you will eat, to shop for ingredients, to cook the meal, set the table, and sit down to eat together. Taking the time to do these things creates a new time: mealtime. Many couples and families who practice the discipline of mealtime find that many of their warmest memories are centered on food and conversation around the table.

Other traditions have to do with the place of individuals within the family structure. In some families, babies are named after relatives; in others, a point is made of giving babies their whole own names. In many families, everyone has an assigned seat at the dinner table, and woe betide any younger brothers who try to sit in their big sisters' chairs. Many families have traditions that commemorate deceased relatives—a yearly visit to the cemetery to care for the family graves; a grandmother's or great-grandmother's powder compact that is carried by all brides.

Physical objects can be important bearers of tradition. Photographs of loved ones, both living and departed, can be reminders of the larger families and communities of which your own marriage and family form a part. A pair of candlesticks, a decorative pillow, a favorite piece of furniture—whether these things are inherited or purchased, they can move with you from your first newlywed apartment through successive dwelling places, helping you to create an ongoing sense of home and family.

Two final elements of tradition that are present in many families are words and humor. Many couples and families have slogans and proverbial expressions and inside jokes that get repeated over and over through the years, and that express and convey the identity and common life of the family. Proverbs and jokes are complex and potentially risky territory, in that it is possible to get into habits that may seem innocuous but are actually quite destructive. Every so often we hear from someone that in his or her family, people say rude things or call each other names, but it's all in fun and is how they show their love for one another. When we hear a story like this, we wonder: if you really do love each other, can't you find another way to show it?

So be sure that your verbal traditions really do express love, and that your jokes really are funny, not only to those who tell them but also to the hearers or the subjects of those jokes. This is not to say that anyone outside the family needs to appreciate your humor or understand what you are talking about. On the contrary—family jokes can be all the funnier for the fact that no one else understands them. They become a kind of code: "We've been together for a long time, and we're still having fun."

A fun-loving spirit can play an important part in carrying a couple through the challenges of family life. "One thing that strikes me about my family is how funny my parents are, and how much fun we've had as a family," wrote one young woman. "When I get married and have a family, I want us to have fun. I want to marry someone who has a good sense of humor and who finds me funny. It seems like it can get you through some really tough stuff."

Bearing Burdens

Inevitably, marriage does involve "tough stuff." But what exactly does that mean? When people say, "Marriage is hard," what do they mean? We can think of at least three possible meanings for this phrase, one false and two true. To begin with the first of these: it is possible that what people mean when they say this is that marriage is hard as compared to other paths in life that are not hard (like singleness, presumably).

We have never heard anyone say this in so many words, but people do sometimes make remarks that come across this way. "Everyone is constantly telling me that marriage is difficult and hard work," wrote a recently married woman. "It really frightens me, because so far, I am enjoying every minute of it. I find myself waiting for the bad times to come, thinking that it will be any day now. Is it really going to get as bad and difficult as people say it is? Should I prepare myself for the worst?"

No, it is not necessary to prepare for the worst just because you got married. Marriage is not a quick way to make your life miserable. It is not a burden that you could have avoided by remaining single, but which you must now do your best to bear up under. Marriage and singleness are different paths in life. There are benefits and drawbacks to either path, but neither one is by definition easier or harder than the other.

On the other hand, there is a sense in which marriage is genuinely hard. One woman wrote,

> My parents' relationship always seems so easy! I said as much to them, and they laughed. My dad explained that the only way they were still happy was because of hours and days and years of hard work. Every day, they have worked at putting the needs of the other before their own, and being willing to give to one another for the betterment of the relationship.

In other words, marriage is hard in the sense that becoming really good at anything is hard. Anyone who plays an instrument well, or is a highly skilled athlete or artist or craftsman, will tell you that the only way he or she attained that level of accomplishment was by working really hard. But fine musicians and artists and athletes are willing to work that hard for that long because they love what they are doing and they want to do it well. That love and that desire make the process as a whole a welcome discipline, even through seasons when it may feel like a long, slow slog.

So also with marriage. Sometimes marital partners feel buoyed up by the delight of their love for one another and the pleasure they take in one another's presence in their lives. At times like these, it is easy to listen patiently, to speak gently, to look for ways to serve one another and to be pleased by one another. And then there are times when none of these things seems easy, when it requires a great deal of discipline to continue to practice the art of treating one another with consideration and respect. This is hard work; so in this sense, yes, marriage is hard.

There is a second sense in which marriage is hard. Marriage is hard because life is hard. Marriage is interwoven with loss and bounded by death, because human life is interwoven with loss and bounded by death. This is why traditional Christian marriage vows read as they do: "I take you as my wedded spouse, for better, for worse, for richer, for poorer, in sickness and in health, to love and to cherish, until we are parted by death."

Christian marriage is not a gamble, whereby we hope that if we choose this person, our future will be marked only by riches, health and living happily ever after. Christian marriage is a promise to love one another in the midst of whatever life brings, recognizing that for the vast majority of us, that means both better and worse, richer and poorer, sickness and health—and recognizing,

too, that we do not have all the time in the world, because death
comes to all of us.

As paradoxical as it may seem, this is good news. It is an invitation to make the most of every day, not taking our loved one's
presence in our lives for granted, not waiting until everything is
perfect to be happy, but rather cherishing the time we have together, even when that time is marked by sorrow or by loss. One
of the things this involves is a willingness to suffer, not in isolation and with our backs turned to one another, but actually with
one another, bearing together whatever burdens life may bring.

We may face the temptation to think of loss as something that
is reserved for the end of life, or at any rate for sometime far in the
future. Of course this is not actually the case. Loss is something
that accompanies all of us throughout our lives. Granted, different
individuals become aware of this in different ways and at different
times. If as a young person you have suffered significant losses,
part of your task in growing up will be to grieve those losses honestly, and thus open yourself to hope. If your early life has been
relatively free of sorrow, part of your task in growing up will be to
learn compassion for those who have suffered in ways you have
not, and to meet your own losses with integrity when they do
come, as they certainly will.

Part of bearing one another's burdens is learning what your partner's burdens are, and being open with your partner about your
own sorrows. You may have suffered in significant ways even before
you met one another. Those losses are part of your stories; they have
shaped the adults you have become, and will continue to affect you
as you move into the future. Sharing your histories of grief with one
another can be an important part of mourning your losses and of
opening yourself to the possibilities that the future holds.

As you talk about past and present losses, you will find that
there is a sense in which your partner's grief becomes yours as

well. This is not to say that you can ever expect to feel a spouse's loss in precisely the same way as he or she does, or that by feeling another's grief deeply you can somehow make his or her sorrow go away. But a grieving spouse is itself an occasion for sorrow, and it may be that your spouse's loss has some direct implications for you as well, as it did for this young woman:

> My fiancé lost his mother several years ago. I did not know him then, and never met her, but her death affects me none-theless. I have realized that one of the things he brings to our relationship is his pain over the death of his mother. He has told me of his sadness that his mother will never know me, and that she will not be here for his college graduation and his wedding. It brings me to tears. I seem to miss a woman I never knew. I wish I had known her; I feel robbed of that op-portunity sometimes.

Spouses may encounter together other burdens in the course of their marriage. An experience shared by many young couples is that of a job-related move to somewhere far from anywhere they have ever lived before. While some couples find this exhilarating, others find it enormously stressful to be removed from supportive networks of relationship with extended family and friends. This is a loss to be mourned, and doing so intentionally and together can help a couple to strengthen their relationship with one another and to find ways in the midst of that loss to begin to build new friendships in their new community.

Another set of losses that are encountered by many couples in their childbearing years are those having to do with pregnancy and childbirth. Infertility, miscarriage, stillbirth and infant death are things people do not talk about much, especially with the young and unmarried or newly married. Most young people sim-ply do not think about infertility. Miscarriage is often a hidden loss, known only to those with whom the bereaved parents choose to share it. And stillbirth and infant death are much, much more rare, at least in modern Western societies, than they once were.

But these losses do happen. The fact is that nobody is guaranteed the ability to conceive, and no pregnancy is guaranteed to end in the delivery of a healthy baby who lives to grow up. Miscarriage is particularly common, and the technological advances (like ultrasound imaging) that can make the experience of pregnancy more vivid can also serve to sharpen the pain of miscarriage, when anticipation of the birth of a child turns into mourning for a child who will not, in fact, be born.

If miscarriage or another pregnancy-related loss does not happen to you, it will happen to a couple you know, and that couple will need your willingness to grieve this loss with them. "We wish that we had known how hard it is to lose a pregnancy, and how often it happens," one man wrote. His wife had recently given birth to their first child, having miscarried two earlier pregnancies. "We had so many people tell us about their loss after we went through it. We had no idea it affected so many people."

There are other burdens that typically arrive in later stages of life: the frustration of realizing that you may never advance as far in your career as you might have wished, for example; or the disorientation of realizing that your children are mostly raised and you are not sure what to do next. And many challenges can arise in any season of life or marriage: financial reversals, health problems, crises or difficulties or losses of whatever kind that affect you or your children or your extended family or your circle of friends.

It is highly unlikely that all of these particular difficulties are going to happen to you, at least not all at once. But it is virtually certain that something hard is going to happen sometime. The health of your marriage will be decisively affected by whether you are able to find ways to bear these burdens together, giving each other space to grieve, and turning toward one another to find ways to cope, and even to thrive, in the midst of it all.

As husbands and wives mourn the burdens that they bear, words and silence and actions will all have a part to play. There are words that do not help people mourn: words like "It's for the best," or "God never gives people more than they can handle," or "Aren't you over that yet?" But there are words that can help: "I'm so sorry," "I don't know why this happened, either," "Would you like to talk about it?" Words like these open doors to the possibility of communication, and of sharing the burden of sorrow with one another.

Silence, too, can be helpful or unhelpful. "I have realized that I have adopted a practice of silence," wrote a woman who had suffered but not yet mourned a great loss. "It is a silence within myself, an ignorance or avoidance of what needs to be healed or restored within myself. It is a silence that aches when it is rubbed, a silence that would bleed if only it were cut open." This was a silence that called out to be broken, to be filled with words or even simply with tears.

But there is a proper silence in the face of sorrow, a silence not of embarrassment or avoidance or disapproval, but of humility and empathy. Silence can be a way of saying, "There is nothing I can do to take away your pain, but I am willing to be with you in your sorrow." Silent presence takes a lot of courage; it can amount to allowing your heart to be broken by the things that break your loved one's heart. But it can be a great gift as well, and one that can facilitate both mourning and healing.

And finally, mourning can include not only talking and listening but also doing. Traditions that allow you to remember loved ones who have preceded you in life and in death can be an important part both of grieving and of healing. Making Easter baskets like the ones your mother always made with you, taking your family hiking the way your father took you when you were a child, remembering the family birthdays and baking each birthday person's favorite cake the way your grandmother used to do—all these can be ways of honoring the memory of your loved one, and of recognizing the continuing influence he or she has in your life.

Bearing Fruit

"I learned more about love this Valentine's Day than I had ever known before," one young woman wrote, a day or two after the holiday. "My boyfriend's grandma passed away this week, so we put aside our dinner plans to go home for the viewing and the funeral. It was a new experience for me to be with him and his family in this time of sorrow. As I saw his grandpa move through the proceedings, seemingly so unsure of what to do without her by his side, it made me think a lot about marriage and what it means to pledge your whole life to someone 'till death do you part.'"

For fifty years this couple had been a team, pouring themselves into a life of service to family, church and community. At the same time, they had both retained their individuality. Throughout the weekend, stories were told about the grandmother, and poems read that she had written. At the funeral, hymns were sung because they were her favorites, and verses read because they were special to her.

"I truly hope that I can find the right balance in my marriage as well," this woman wrote. "I want to find that balance between keeping one's own 'self' and also becoming one with another. I am grateful for this tangible example of what lifelong commitment looks like, and also the reminder of how short and precious our time is here. I hope that I live life the way she did, leaving lasting fruit behind from a life lived in the presence of God."

Every marriage is different. Every individual is unique, and the marriages that particular partners create with one another are unique as well. It can take time, therefore, to see what kind of fruit your marriage may bear, because it will not be exactly the same as the fruit of anyone else's marriage. Of course one expects to see some common threads in all successful marriages: respect, intimacy, forgiveness, commitment, an appreciation of the blessings that have come to your particular family over time. But what exactly will this look like for you?

You don't have to know ahead of time. In order to raise a child well, you do not have to decide that the baby is going to grow up to be a pastor or a plumber, a nurse or an engineer. It is enough to receive the baby thankfully, rear him or her thoughtfully and compassionately, and wait to see how and where God will lead your child over the course of his or her life.

And so also in marriage. In order to be married well, you do not have to decide ahead of time exactly what your marriage is going to look like fifty years from now. It is enough that you are open to whatever the years may bring, and that you nurture your life together as it grows, little by little, from its beginnings into maturity.

No marriage is exciting all of the time. All marriages are hard some of the time. And very few people who have been successfully married for many years would want it any other way. The exhilaration and exuberance and intensity of young love are good things. The settled calm that comes with having weathered many storms together is at least as good. Together, you can become people you never would have been apart from each other, partners in a marriage that has grown from young love into the complexity and maturity that is old love.

Epilogue

Weddings

WHY DO PEOPLE HAVE WEDDINGS? After all, you don't have to have a wedding in order to get married. You can get married in the pastor's study with a couple of friends to serve as witnesses, and at the end of the day you're just as married as if you had spent the $25,000 on your wedding that is now the average in contemporary America, or the $150,000 to $200,000 that is charged by top-of-the-line wedding planners in trendy locations.[1]

Probably one reason you are having a wedding is that your parents would be disappointed if you didn't. "My mother has dreamed about my wedding for longer than I have," wrote one bride-to-be. "It would absolutely have crushed her if we had refused my parents' offer to give us a wedding." The rest of your family and friends may also be expecting a certain kind of celebration. "There is a sense in which you feel obligated to throw a big party," wrote an engaged man. "There are standards for what you do at a wedding, and if you don't do it, you feel that you are letting people down."

And it may be that you, too, want a party, as this young man did:

---

[1]Laura M. Holson, "With This Burger, I Thee Wed," *New York Times,* June 16, 2009.

I'd like to have a big wedding. When I get married, I want all of my friends and family there with my bride and me to celebrate. I want my bride to have the long, flowing white gown and a whole fleet of bridesmaids and flower girls. At the reception I want a huge feast with tons of delicious food, lots of music and dancing, and lots of laughing and celebrating. It's not because I want to compete with anyone else. It's not because I want to show off. I want to have an incredible wedding because I believe that events that special are worth celebrating wholeheartedly.

We have no wish to pour cold water on anyone's desire for a wedding. Marriage is indeed worth celebrating. But we do think it is important to make two points. First, most people cannot afford the lavish wedding that is now the touchstone of American consumer culture.[2] Price tags are not part of most people's wedding fantasies, but they are most definitely a part of wedding reality. "It's certainly not what you dream about as a little girl," wrote one bride. "In that dream, the ceremony, reception, flowers and photography all come together flawlessly. You never think about questions like, 'Where are we going to get the money to afford all this?'"

Second, there is tremendous pressure to spend lavishly on a wedding even when you can't afford it, because lavish weddings have become the magic charm by which bridal couples and their families assure themselves and everybody else that their past and present and future are all perfect. So important is the lavish wedding that the world of wedding advice is full of pointers on how to look like you have spent lavishly even if you haven't: buy the designer gown on clearance, have your formal dinner on some day other than Saturday, and so forth. No one ever says, wear your

---

[2]On this subject see Cele C. Otnes and Elizabeth H. Pleck, *Cinderella Dreams: The Allure of the Lavish Wedding* (Berkeley: University of California Press, 2003).

Sunday best, serve your guests cake and punch in the church hall, and call it a day. Why not? Because such an event would not look expensive, and a proper wedding, so it is supposed, has to either be expensive or look expensive.[3]

We should hardly have to point out that there is nothing in Christian tradition to suggest that it is important to have a lavish wedding. The out-of-season flowers flown in from halfway around the world, the row of groomsmen in identical rented tuxedos, the pew bows, the videographer, the monogrammed napkins and matchbooks, the party favor bubbles in individual church-shaped containers, the doves and butterflies and balloons—they are all artifacts of a culture whose twin idols are romance and consumerism and in which weddings are an opportunity to bow down at both of these altars at once. No amount of evangelizing in the wedding homily can obscure the fact that at most American weddings, it is Mammon who is most obviously being worshiped.

Christian tradition does, however, suggest that an authentic human and Christian life is a life in community. Yes, you could elope (or be married in the pastor's study), and we have heard more than a few engaged couples say they wish they felt they could do so. If the pressure from family and friends to make overly elaborate, overly expensive plans becomes too great, the pastor's study really might be your best option. After all, you don't want to spend your marriage caving in to pressure from others to spend beyond your means. Why start out with a wedding of which that is true?

It is possible to have a wedding that is not lavish, though. For most couples, a modest wedding is preferable to a private ceremony, precisely because it is a wedding. It is an opportunity for the family and friends of the bride and groom to gather in support

---

[3]See, for example, "Eight Ways to Reduce the Average Cost of a Wedding," June 11, 2008 <www.smartmoney.com/personal-finance/marriage-divorce/theyll-never-know -eight-hidden-ways-to-cut-wedding-costs-13918/>.

and celebration of this new couple and their new marriage, and to step together into a future in which these two have become one. If this is the reason you are having a wedding, it may well be possible to come up with plans for a meaningful ceremony and celebration that are both lovely and affordable. Such a wedding will most likely look like you did not spend a fortune, and that will be fine, because you didn't.

To put it another way: a good wedding is a wedding that participates in the reality of your life, rather than representing a departure from it. A wedding in which you are the prince and princess of the day is only good if you really are royalty. If you're not, it's a costume party, not a wedding. Let your wedding be a celebration of your life, of your history and your hopes, not somebody else's.

Your life includes a lot of other people, and so will your wedding and the process of planning for it. Negotiating the details of the wedding with other key stakeholders—including most particularly the parents of the bride and groom—is typically the most stressful part of wedding planning.[4] Bridal couples and their parents can easily find themselves engaged in conversations that resemble a game of tug of war, with the bride and groom playing the part of the rope.

The more you can do to make wedding planning a cooperative enterprise, the happier you all are likely to be, both with the process and with the end result. Don't say, "It's my day, and I should have what I want." Instead say, "This is an important event for all of us, and we need to work together to make plans that fit for all of us." If the bride and groom can do this with each other and with each of their families, they will have taken important first steps toward learning to work together as a couple and toward manag-

---

[4]For an excellent resource on using wedding planning as an opportunity to grow relationships, see William Doherty and Elizabeth Doherty Thomas, *Take Back Your Wedding: Managing the People Stress of Wedding Planning* (BookSurge, 2007).

ing boundaries and expectations with their extended families, steps that can only help all of these relationships to develop in positive ways in the future.

Your life also includes sadness as well as joy, and you will be more likely to be able to plan and celebrate a joyful wedding if you make room for sorrow. You may find very bittersweet the process of planning a wedding that some important person did not live to see. Your parents may be wondering where the years went, and feeling keenly the passing of the day when you were a small child and they were all the world to you. Your siblings and friends and you yourself may be mourning the passing of your single days, even as all of you look forward to this new season of life.

A properly Christian wedding has room for mixed feelings, whether these are yours or anybody else's. Christian weddings are not showcases of mythical perfection. A Christian wedding is a parable, an everyday event that offers a glimpse of the world that God created and is recreating, a world in which human sorrows and limitations and possibilities are gathered up and renewed and redeemed, not by purchased illusions of perfection, but by God himself.

So plan a wedding that isn't perfect. Have a short engagement, so that you have fewer options to begin with and less time in which to be caught up in wedding mania. Be honest with yourselves and with your families about what you can afford, and then live within your limitations. Ask a friend to make the dress or bake the cake. Put a candle on the altar or a flower on the piano in memory of a loved one who has died. And then celebrate your wedding day surrounded by people who care about you and who pray God's blessing on you.

Subject index

grandparents. *See* parents
grief
  for deceased loved ones, 9, 63, 212,
    217, 220, 227
  God's, 32, 69, 75
  for infertility, 161
  part of life, 33, 56, 62, 184, 201, 210
  for pregnancy loss, 218
  sharing, 74-75, 120, 216-20
  at weddings, 227
hooking up, 14-15, 17, 21, 115, 130
hospitality
  beyond the family circle, 166, 173
  and children, 40, 154, 172-74
  as dimension of the kingdom of God,
    172
  in family life, 73-74
  and food, 168, 174
  and limits, 78
  and perfection, 168
  and privacy, 153
humans as male and female, 14, 41-42, 46,
  90, 93, 95, 155
illness and disability, 29, 42, 149
infertility, 161, 183, 217
infidelity. *See* adultery
intimacy
  between mothers and infants, 171
  with God, 22-23
  and hospitality, 73, 153
  with people, 27, 29, 105-7, 112, 174
  relationship to romance, 23, 25, 27, 29,
    109
  as requiring mutual presence, 116-20
  as requiring self-disclosure, 61,
    120-24, 126
  tempting shortcuts, 117-18
  and time for oneself, 207-8
  and trustworthiness, 116
  See also friendship and sex
Jesus
  and discipleship, 31, 33, 62, 71, 132
  and divorce, 47
  and the family, 43, 69-71, 156
  and God the Father, 94
  and hospitality, 74
  as lover, 25-26
  and marriage, 38, 48
  and money, 184-85
  and peace, 82-83
  and power, 93
  and the words of institution, 59
  See also God

justice, in family life, 75-76, 78, 181
living together. *See* cohabitation
love
  being in, 127, 138, 202-203
  as creative, 166
  delaying, 14, 17
  disappointment in, 28
  as excuse for bad behavior, 85-86, 103
  falling in and out of, 22
  in families, 58, 66, 77, 197
  fathers and, 63
  and friendship, 105-6
  as gift of self, 45
  of God, 33, 57, 151, 157, 165
  and honesty, 30, 67
  and hospitality, 73
  of Jesus, 25-26
  letters, 23-24, 128
  and marriage, 12, 39, 42, 90, 94, 111,
    176
  mature, 200-201
  mothers and, 203
  need for, 170
  perfect, 19-25
  real, 27-32
  and safety, 55-56
  and sex, 133
  showing, 193, 213
  True Love Waits, 132
  and wisdom, 31
  young, 19, 203, 221
Luther, Martin, 32, 49
male-female relationships
  consensus, 100-101
  control, 56, 82, 85-88, 91, 93, 95-97
  doctrine of separate spheres, 179
  egalitarianism, 96-97
  gender roles, 90-97, 179
  headship, 91-97
  intrinsic to marriage, 41-42, 46, 155
  leadership, 91-93
  mutuality, 52, 94, 97, 190
  power, 65, 76, 82, 90, 93, 95-97, 104,
    130, 189-90
  submission, 69, 86-87, 93-95
  teamwork, 97, 99, 102, 167, 188,
    220
marriage
  as embodied, 45-46, 137
  historical perspectives on, 36-49, 53
  as optional, 12, 43-45
  as sacrament, 38
miscarriage. *See* pregnancy loss

Scripture index